The End Times

A Spiritual Survival Kit For The Last Days

Kristina Murawski

Cover designed by:

The name of the fallen angel, is intentionally, not capitalized throughout this book, unless it is at the beginning of a sentence or used as shown in a scripture reference.

Kristina Murawski

ISBN: 9780578669410
ISBN-13: 978-0-578-66941-0

DEDICATION

This book is dedicated to Yeshua Hamashiac,
my Friend, Father, and my God.

I sought the Lord

And he answered me;

He delivered me from all my fears.

Psalm 34:4 (NIV)

ACKNOWLEDGMENTS

I would like to start by saying thank you to Yeshua Hamashiac for assigning this book to me. Without His instructions, it would not be in existence today.

I would also like to thank my daughter Zipporah, and her father Stephen for their profound love and support.. You are both, day-in and day-out, the most important people in my life.

In honoring my parents, I want to thank you for your constant support to pursue my dreams.

I would like to acknowledge the following people who have encouraged me throughout the writing of this book, and my walk with Christ. You have helped to keep me grounded with wisdom and love throughout this process and otherwise. Zipporah Marley, Stephen Marley, Mary Murawski, Allen Murawski, Kent and Gina Murawski, Tim and Maria Wolf, Gina Dennison, Nina LLopis, Melissa Bashor, Kerrie Mitchell and Denvil and Krista Lee.

Spiritual Survival Kit for the End Times

TABLE OF CONTENTS

FOREWARD

The author, Kristina Murawski, accepted Christ into her life when she was a teenager. It was many years later before she came to the realization that Jesus wanted to have a relationship with her. Although each of us have our own personal journey in our walk with Him, Kristina attempts to capture what the Lord has done in her life as she shares an important message that God has placed on her heart. There are times when God asks her to go into places of darkness to reach the lost. They may never set foot into a church. God also is speaking to Kristina about the uncertain times that we live in. God is reaching out to this world, and using people like Kristina to sound a warning. Take heed and prepare, for He is coming back soon!

Kristina Murawski

1 YOUR BIBLE IS YOUR BLUEPRINT TO HEAVEN

Salvation as we know it, is to be saved. Saved from what? Saved from whom? This indicates that we must be in dire need of something or someone to take us from our imminent disaster or pending destruction; to be removed from that which torments us or our lives. This is exactly true. What is it that we need to be saved from?

We not only need saving from ourselves and our adversaries, but also, for the benefits to our extended lives or after lives as we know them.

Each and every purposeful thought and act of obedience to Jesus Christ is a step closer to our purpose of being fulfilled for His Kingdom. We may take a moment or two out of our long days to thank God for something, but how often do we stop to listen to what he is saying to us? It is imperative to know God's voice. It is one of the most important privileges of knowing Him, besides worshipping Him, that we will need in general, but also for the end-times. In these days, it will be dark, cold, scary, and desolate.

If we are wandering around the world, lost in translation somewhere, or caught up in the world's behaviors, what then will we do when confronted with our persecutors? What then will we do when confronted with the evil that is unseen, yet they're watching every move that we make? The very demons that will try to kill us and our children will be stronger than ever. They will be looking to kill and destroy with might! They will come in sheep's clothing; they will come as light. Jesus Christ, and His word are the way, to not only a beautiful, long lasting, fulfilling relationship, but also to having the authority of His power to conquer all obstacles placed in our way. He loves us so much, but He will always be glorified no matter what we do or don't do. He is deserving of all praise, all glory, and all submission. If you aren't aware of this now, you will be. I only pray that it is before He comes. I pray that it is done willingly. I pray it will be today.

As 2 Corinthians 11:14 (ESV) states ***And no wonder, for even satan disguises himself as an angel of light.*** One of his goals will be to deceive us into thinking that he is good, loving, and powerful. Naturally, because we are created from the Lord who is love, we as humans are drawn to light. Satan knows this and understands that to draw a massive number of people into the kingdom of darkness, he must, once again, imitate God to achieve this goal. But what is ever so important to understand, is that the Bible, the Holy Word of God, the very breath of our Father, must be tattooed on our hearts to survive. Let's look at Isaiah 8: 20-22 (NLT):

> ***Look to God's instructions and teachings! People who contradict his word are completely in the dark. They will go from one place to another, weary and hungry. And because they are hungry, they will rage and curse their king and their God. They will look up to heaven and down at the earth, but wherever they look, there will be trouble and anguish and dark despair.***

They will be thrown out into the darkness.

So let's get something straight here. In order for people to contradict His word to be in complete darkness, one must first know His word. And to look up to heaven and down at the earth, they must understand that heaven exists. This is a warning for God's people! The bride! We must pay close attention to following His instructions, as they will save our very lives, catapulting us into eternity with Him in all of His glory! Let us remember that even though I will be talking about satan, his strategies, and how to fight the enemy, that Jesus the Messiah, has already won! This book is meant to encourage and teach, while also adhering to some discipline, that is guided by the word of God. He will parent us as we parent our children, and at times it is uncomfortable, but oh so necessary.

Having said all of that, let's continue now with understanding that the Bible is the tool that will keep us well equipped for the war. It is the very tool that will save us from our adversaries. It is the very tool that will help us discern from the light and the dark in the end. The written out, printed word of God is not the only tool we will use, but it is definitely a significant one.

There have been times in the last couple of years that God spoke to me about the importance of having printed copies of a Bible, not only the online or app versions that we may have on our phones and computers. He explained to me that there will come a day when having a phone, computer, television, or any electronics at all, will be dangerous or non-existent. He showed me that the pages and pages of notes from my studying of the Bible that I have hand written were actually direct advice He had given me long ago. I wasn't aware at the time that this was His wisdom, but later in life when He began to prepare me more, He also pointed this truth out to me. In response to this truth, years later, when I began Bible College, instead of taking notes and making outlines on any device, I decided to hand-write each and every one.

To me, it seems quite impossible to have the entire Bible memorized word for word, but what will we do if every Bible is forcefully taken from us? What will we do if every sermon we have every preached, listened to, or have taken notes on, is digitally saved? I am not saying that I am living in the dark ages, but I am saying that paper versions of these things will be necessary. From the things that He has shown me, we will need to have scripture memorized, and a few different Bibles tucked away in safe places. He has stated clearly that if there are any pastors and preachers that believe they will be teaching in the end times, they should begin writing all of their information out, or all of their work for future reference should be printed and archived in a safe place.

Are you aware that many prophetic words written in the Bible have come to pass and those that have not yet, definitely will? Did you know that there are a few books in the Bible that speak on exactly what the end of the world will look like? They tell what will happen to people who believe in Jesus Christ, and also the people who don't believe in Him. The Bible explains how things will look in the years prior to the end of time. The prophets in the Bible described the natural disasters, the wars and which nations will be involved. These words written thousands of years ago, tell us exactly what we will be battling in this time. Yet it seems many people in our world are ignorant of the power in this word. It seems that there are some that ignore it completely and follow other teachings, while some people take bits and pieces of the Bible, along with other books, to form their own interpretation of life.

For those of you that don't believe in the Bible, I would challenge you to begin reading it, and for those of you that do, I would challenge you to begin believing it. We must study this word because it is what will keep us alive in the years to come. I realize you may be thinking I am over exaggerating here, however, the Bible proves itself time and time again to be true, and embodying such powerful truth that without it and the wisdom it offers, we will be destroyed.

God has put such an urgency on my heart and for my ministry concerning the end times and deliverance, that it would be of utmost disobedience for me to ignore it. Unfortunately within time, one by one, humans will be deceived by the devil and wiped off this earth. This is not exaggerating. This is not a strong opinion. It is a fact. The very blueprint that maps out your survival, at-least in the USA, is as easy to buy as a pack of gum. How blessed we are today to have this opportunity to read the future at hand to prepare ourselves and our families. We as a people, and we as a body, must begin looking at the bigger picture now. If we have been avoiding this, consider yourself blessed that you have today to pray. Consider yourself blessed that you have today to give Jesus your life. Consider yourself blessed that you have today to spiritually prepare for what is to come.

He has told me to take care of the information that He has helped me gather over the years, as well as my Bibles. To keep them protected and in secure locations with secure storage devices. Some think it's important to store your money in a bank, or have some off-shore account, and I would say beware of storing your treasures here on earth, but if you must, make your treasures that which would please God. It is Him you will answer to one day, so it is Him we should aim to please. What will please God is your survival through the times of despair. Although there will be an equal amount of revival and light along with this demise, there is a clear path as to which team you will be on. He cares so much for us that He planned at the beginning of time to put His words on paper for us to read so that we could prepare for the inevitable demise of satan, and the inevitable triumph of Christ! We must use wisdom and discernment with such powerful information. To guard your Bibles as if they were worth millions of dollars will be the very attitude that will help save you and your family from evil.

I would like to share a dream God once gave me. I do rely on some of my dreams as prophetic warnings, and teachings. Sometimes they are so clear and so precise that when they happen in reality, I am usually not surprised. I am however, always intrigued by God's awesomeness to communicate things to me before they happen. This dream in particular was ignited by a question that was looming in my heart for months before. I didn't understand the scripture found in Matthew referring to the elect.

It states ***For false messiahs and false prophets will appear and perform great signs and wonders to deceive, if possible, even the elect.*** Matthew 24:24 (NIV).

How can this happen? How can we lovers of Christ be deceived in this time when false messiahs and false prophets will appear? Surely we are well versed biblically! Surely we are close enough to Christ to hear and heed to his instruction! This is where my desire for putting this puzzle together started.

God began to show me slowly, day after day, how the mark of the beast and the deceit will correlate in this time. I will speak in depth on the mark of the beast in a later chapter, but I wanted to preface the warning of this dream with a known connection of the two. In my dream God showed me an aerial view of the antichrist and the false prophet plotting their attack together. They had their own book with the strategy they were going to use. Then I was placed in a city that symbolized the whole world where a huge dragon clothed in light blue silk soared around the city. People were cheering as this ginormous creature paraded around looking beautiful and glorious. Its size alone was enough to leave any human in awe. But then on top of that, it had an innocence about it, and a splendor. I was shocked at the people who ran to see it. I was dumbfounded at the people that were praising this giant beast clothed in innocence.

When I awoke from the dream, God spoke very clearly that this monster masquerading around in goodness and holiness was exactly how it will happen. The beast will come as light, clothed in innocence, brilliance, and size, deceiving all with its power and beauty. Don't think for one moment that the Bible's explanation of this deception is wrong. Year after year the Bible proves itself to skeptics and scientist alike to be true in its entirety. He will come in light and deceive many. I don't like to reference scripture too much out of context, however in this case I feel it is important that you can understand that without knowledge we will be destroyed. In Hosea chapter 4:1b-6 (NIV), it gives a better idea to that which I am referring:

"There is no faithfulness, no love, no acknowledgment of God in the land. There is

> *only cursing, lying and murder, stealing and adultery; they break all bounds, and bloodshed follows bloodshed. Because of this the land dries up, and all who live in it waste away; the beasts of the field, the birds in the sky and the fish in the sea are swept away.*
> *But let no one bring a charge, let no one accuse another, for your people are like those who bring charges against a priest. You stumble day and night, and the prophets stumble with you. So I will destroy your mother. My people are destroyed from lack of knowledge. Because you have rejected knowledge, I also reject you as my priests; because you have ignored the law of your God, I also will ignore your children."*

"My people are destroyed from lack of knowledge." What a statement! We cannot afford to live in a lie. We cannot afford to live without seeking this knowledge that God is speaking of here. If we are not prepared spiritually, in our minds as well as our spirits, it will be our demise; hence why I have devoted many years of study, research and time to the Lord, and will continue until his return.

As each year passes here on earth, I notice that more and more people are steering away from the Word of God because it doesn't suit their lifestyle choices. I have also noticed people standing up for loved ones' choices so much so that they themselves have been affected in an ungodly way. So with each passing year, the people of God make one more compromise for a friend or family member, or a circumstance that they feel is appropriate. They do this all in the name of love.

God is love, so it may feel right at times to support a friend or spouse in an attempt to show the very love of God. I get it. And sometimes this is correct, but never when it means going against the will of God. How do we know when it goes against His will? If the Bible says it, or if He says it to us. So we have to know and read the word, as well as have a relationship with Him to understand and discern. Also, deliverance from demons is very helpful at these moments when confusion hits. There is a very thin line between loving others with our hearts and brokenness, and loving others with the mighty love of God.

It seems that satan likes to deceive people with a lie of what love really is. He does this with the help of his demons. He begins by lying to you about God's love for you. It is easy to believe his lies if we don't yet know, live, and breathe God's true love for us, hence it is important to have an on-going personal intimate relationship with Him.

It can be a circumstantial position in which you are born into a family that doesn't know the love of the Father, therefore imparting the opposite spirit in your life. Or, one can develop this lie throughout the years, having trauma, unfortunate happenings, or long suffering. Also, there are times that it is ingrained in your bloodline and genetics. Therefore, through no fault of your own, this tight grip of a lie is just living in you. All of these reasons for the lie to infiltrate our lives are very legitimate sources of never truly understanding the love of Jesus. But fear not, He will continue to pursue you with His everlasting love.

Thankfully we have a God that never, ever gives up on us. There are many people, and many testimonies of this. Even in my own life, God was so taken with love for me that He introduced himself to me. Yet when I slowly turned away from Him, year after year, by the seductions of the world, He continued to pursue me. Thankfully, I heard His call years later. After being a backslidden, lukewarm Christian that led to a numbness to His very presence, one would think there was no salvation to come. But that isn't God, the Creator. He makes a way for everyone to know His love if we are willing.

We must look with a magnifying glass at the future we will all face. We must hone into the problems that lie deep within our souls, flesh and minds to win the battle of love. If children grow up watching television shows that have magical love spells of wonder, and happily ever after endings, we are going to have teenagers who turn to psychics and mediums for advice and partake of love spell rituals of their own. We are going to have teenagers become adults that pursue new- age strategies such as reiki healings, yoga, stones, spirit guides, shamans, or worse.

I am sorry if any of you reading this engage in any of these practices, but if you continue to read, you will see the horrific dangers that each of these practices can bring. Each one of these avenues attracts certain demons. People are innocently searching for answers, happy endings, healing and love, but in return have temporary relief and a slew of demons chasing after them. Satan is here to kill and destroy; he will deceive you in any way possible. It is how he does this, that in my opinion, is so generic it makes me cringe. He uses our weaknesses.

For example, if love is all that we desire; a marriage, a husband to dote over our every need, or a man to be the king over you, then it is love he will use to destroy you and bring you closer to the dark side with hoping to keep you there. If alcohol is a problem that runs in your family, he will do his best to get you drinking at a young age to begin his path of destruction for you. If it is a sexual problem that plagues your family, whether it be having numerous partners, plural marriage, sexual abuse or otherwise, he will make sure that you are molested, introduced to pornography or prostitution, or have an overall disturbing experience to distort your perception of sexual things at a young age. He also will find a way to glorify sex and place it upon a pedestal for you to strive to accomplish having many women or men. He will make it his business for you to make sex number one in your life causing sex to become your god.

What if it is health that calls you? An optimistic, healthy exercise regime each day is a beneficial thing in life. We must take care of the bodies God has given us to house His Spirit, however, I have seen satan bring people to the opposite side of the spectrum. He digs deep to find that this exercise can easily become an obsession to you because vanity has corrupted your soul. He does this by using a form of gluttony. I will touch upon this further in the chapter of demons. With all of the celebrities looking perfect, how could vanity not play a role in our lives. But you're innocently just "taking care of your body" right? Yet people somehow end up making exercise and healthy living their god, having now given in to satan's plan.

Satan knows the word of God better than we do. He spends his time accusing us of our wrongs. We must smarten up and arn the word of God. We must learn it and speak it, sing it, shout it, proclaim it, declare it, and obey it. When we do this, within a matter of time, we will begin to live it. We will begin to walk as Christ did and follow His instructions. But all of these little deceptions, whether it be psychics, magic, yoga, third eye, or black magic, white magic, addictions, obsessions, or even a deceptive type of love, will not only delay us from having the revelation of God's love, but can sometimes hinder us from ever seeing it.

For all who are reading this book, let me ask you, did you pick it up because the title is catchy? Or did you pick it up because the end of the world discussions intrigue you or scare you? Do you secretly enjoy that hint of mystery and fear? I'm quite sure that God himself wanted each and every person that reads this book, to read it and receive all the revelation within it. So perhaps you won't be too quick to judge the strong truths that are displayed in this book, but that you will take each word of knowledge to heart; after all, it could save your life.

I do not know your background, I do not know your mother and father or how they raised you. I do not know your religious beliefs or disbeliefs, but what I do know is that the end is near, and if you are not prepared, you will spend eternity, a very very long, permanent life in misery and agony separated from the love of God. I do not say this to scare you, or act as though my God is a dreadful scary man in the sky, rather, I say it because He has shown me bits of both heaven and hell. I assure you, it was so profound, that it would be a travesty to keep it from any human alive. So, my friends, take the time to finish the book and chew on the words, for it is a life and death situation with which we are faced. Life eternally, or death eternally, that is the question. Let's not dismiss the tool God gave us to be equipped for His return. Instead, let's study the Holy blueprint He provided for us and be excellent stewards of God.

2 GAINING POWER

When we observe the word lukewarm, what does it bring to mind? Perhaps it is when we turn the faucet on at the kitchen sink and stand there for a moment testing the water with our finger to make sure it isn't too hot, or too cold. Or how about when a dear friend gives you half-hearted support with an issue you are having? Do you think of them as a "lukewarm" friend? Where is your passion in life? Does it rest upon the love you have for your children? Does it rest within the security of your job that keeps you comfortable in life? Does it rest within a skill or talent that you hold? These are all gifts in life. Having passion in our lives is very necessary to perseverance and strength, however, today I want to touch upon having passion for something that will matter after you die. This is a selfless passion that needs to be sought out, as it was created in you before you were even formed in your mother's womb. This is a passion that has nothing to do with your own desires, gifts, or talents, yet everything to do with the Creator's purpose for your life. When we do this half-heartedly, or possibly not at all, it is something that needs correcting immediately. When addressing such a topic as being lukewarm in our own lives, we have to look at all facets of the understanding of the adjective, and also the spiritual side effects.

Let us begin with the scripture. In my interpretation

of Revelation 3:15-19 (NLT) Jesus is not only correcting us in our lack of enthusiasm for His purpose, His teachings, and the gospel itself, but also showing us how much he loves us by informing us of how we can see, be unashamed, and rich in Him. The scripture reads:

> ***"I know all the things you do, that you are neither hot nor cold. I wish that you were one or the other! But since you are like lukewarm water, neither hot nor cold, I will spit you out of my mouth! You say 'I am rich. I have everything I want. I don't need a thing!' And you don't realize that you are wretched and miserable and poor and blind and naked. So I advise you to buy gold from me-gold that has been purified by fire. Then you will be rich. Also buy white garments from me so you will not be shamed by your nakedness, and ointment for your eye so you will be able to see. I correct and discipline everyone I love. So be diligent and turn from your indifference."***

At this point in the scripture, He is speaking to the church in Laodicea in the book of Revelation. This was the seventh church He was addressing with correction. It was also the only church that Christ did not commend for anything. They seemed to have fallen away, and become complacent in their dealings with their faith in Christ and His message. They were materially wealthy wanting and needing for nothing, at least as far as the flesh and world are concerned. However, Jesus was not okay with this mentality. He is calling those who feel they have all they need, deluded in their faith, miserable, poor, blind, and naked. They have lost all of their power. Regardless of what they think, they are on a slow decline to satan's house.

Jesus is teaching us here how important it is for us to understand His purification in our lives. Christ is using gold that has been purified by fire, as a metaphor for His refining of our souls. Again, I think we should look at the word refine to grasp exactly what he is getting at here. Becoming refined is a process of purification used to eliminate unwanted elements. The definition of the verb to refine is to "remove impurities or unwanted elements from (a substance), typically as part of an industrial process." And according to ***New Wilson's Old Testament Word Studies***[1] it means "to strain, to filter, to melt, to try, to purify by fire." According to Malachi 3:3 (NIV):

> ***"He will sit as a refiner and purifier of silver; he will purify the Levites and refine them like gold and silver. Then the Lord will have men who will bring offerings in righteousness,"***

The "gold" or soul that we receive from Him are all of these things, but the gold we currently have is actually a misfortune. It can be difficult for some to look realistically at their lives and see any view that isn't a worldly one. A worldly view of refinement means to have money, power, and success. It means to have conquered your fears, achieved your goals, and risen high above all that once told you that you would never amount to anything. Our world will somehow find a way to shine praises down upon you if you have worldly success, money, and power. Although this can be a positive thing and a blessing straight from God, this passion we are to embody isn't about us.

Sanctification is to walk holy and righteous with Him that will judge us. It is to walk as Christ walked on earth, doing as He did, healing as He did, and casting out demons as He did. Jesus' refinement is surrendering every bit of who you are to Him and allowing Him to burn away that which is not of Him. It is a process of shedding that which doesn't serve God.

More often than not, I see Jesus remove any ungodly love for money, self- achievement, a competitive spirit, and worldly power during the process of refinement. But when this occurs, we become the most powerful that we have ever been. We become the richest on the planet. We become meek with understanding, compassion and humility. We finally embody the very righteousness and authority that was given so freely to us. We begin to wear the righteous and authoritative spirit of Jesus. I realize that those that have not yet been through the refining fire of God may view it as human weakness, unintelligent, or even unpreparedness, but the truth is, it is the exact opposite of this.

Satan purposely offers you distractions to keep you from walking in God's purpose for your life. He will try to give you feelings of jealousy or inadequacy to entice you to strive for the top of that corporate ladder. He will deliberately push you further and further away from that which matters for your eternal life. He will keep you blinded in this short time while here on earth. For the most part, satan has completely overtaken all media and television productions so that he can distract us from what is really going on in the world.

We need to begin to allow the Holy Spirit to open our eyes and refine and shape the parts of our beings that we cannot see; the soul and spirit. I say often to people I love that this life is short so we had better live it with purpose and determination, for the Kingdom of Heaven, and nothing else. It may seem easier said than done, but not really. When we allow Jesus to take over and refine us, He does it, and He does it so well, that you may not even recognize the strength and righteousness in you, but you will know who you are more than ever. You will learn how to gain all the power you need to walk in your path.

So let's discuss for a moment the process of refining a metal in hopes of giving you a picture of why God does what He does. To summarize what June Hill so eloquently described in *A Letter form June on Trials*.[2] The first step of a refiner is to break open the rough ore. Why do you suppose they begin by breaking open this drab, dull piece of matter? This is because inside there is a beautifully precious material deep within it. If it were never broken open, then perhaps the secret of the beauty and the value that were inside would never be known due to the outer encasing of plain, misshapen, piece of garbage. It is important to see the symbolism Christ uses with the refining process to understand what will be happening in our lives. Not that we are dull hunks of junk, but rather showing our imperfections in our flesh.

How many of you can say that there is nothing on your body that you would prefer to be a little different? A smaller nose perhaps? A smaller tummy? Less wrinkles? I think as human beings we are tough critics on our outer appearance due to media propaganda of what perfection looks like. This too, is an easy distraction from that which is inside of us. If we could rate how our souls look, somehow gaining the ability to judge whether it is beautiful or not, it would put our lives into a realistic perspective. But there is no such meter. There is no such tool that can do that except for Holy

Spirit Himself. And the good thing here is that He removes what He knows wasn't there when He created us. He takes from you everything that will hurt you in anyway in the short or long run. He destroys that which is trying to destroy you because He loves you and you are His creation. So my point here is that the "us" on the outside is not the same as the "us" on the inside. Our spirit is where Christ's Spirit dwells, and that spirit cannot be seen just by looking at our fleshly bodies.

The second step of a refiner is to put the unrefined ingredient, perhaps silver, into a crucible. The refiner puts broken, crushed ore into a "crucible"—a fireproof melting pot able to withstand extreme heat. Then the refiner places the crucible into the furnace at the precise temperature necessary for removing other metals that would take away or taint the quality of the gold or silver.

This part of the process in our lives would be taking that which makes up our character and moral value or theologies and cleansing them. Washing away the debris built up after many years of trials and experiences can take time and a clear execution. Have you ever used a dirty rag to wash a car? It is inevitable that the dirt from the rag would then transfer to the car, thus giving you a dirtier car than that which you began. This step in the process is imperative in order to prepare us for having noble intentions and proper motives in our walk with Christ. When you are a part of the church body, you must have God's number one motive in mind when walking with Christ, and that is His Glory. There are many wonderful things about God but the most important is for Him to receive all of His splendor in Glory. This can happen when our character is fully cleansed by the refining fire.

In the third step in the refinement process we can refer to Proverbs 25:4 (NIV) ***Remove the dross from***

the silver, and the silversmith can produce a vessel;.

To be passive and indifferent is sinful. This chapter is not meant for condemnation, or for judgment, rather for growth of the body of Christ. This burning away of sins and transforming more and more into Christ is something that must occur for the body to have true salvation. A true walk with Christ consists of becoming like Christ.

When God speaks to me about the body, one of the things He shares with me is the lack of selflessness. The same humble spirit that once hung on a cross, was spit at, mocked, whipped with sharp razors and eventually sacrificed, was the same spirit that allowed it to happen with all of heaven at His fingertips. At any moment during the crucifixion, Jesus could have easily stopped it. However, He endured it to the end, with a selfless love for us. He endured it to the end with an ultimate purpose for us. Because of His death, we are set free from every curse, every illness, every sin, every shame, every lack.

I feel strongly that we as the church body cannot walk in this fullness without understanding first the importance of being one-hundred and fifty percent full of Christ. How can we do this if we are still walking around in passivity about the kingdom? It is a passivity about spreading the amazing good news that we can all be saved from these things that keep us in bondage? We cannot do this until we gain revelation of the importance of praying for a supernatural portion of God's faith to be instilled in us. It can then penetrate our hearts, catapulting us into the revelatory understanding of what it means to be a Christian in this day and age. If we know doctrine and truth, but mask all of our sins with an over exaggeration of grace, or bypass sin because we are not to judge, are we walking in Christ's Kingdom? Can we ask Him for forgiveness for all of the things we have done to hurt Him? Can we ask Him to search our hearts and reveal the hidden sin deep within us? Can we surrender ourselves to His mission? If we can find it in ourselves to give Him complete permission to transform our lives, no matter what it will look like in the process, He will do it. And in return, you will have gained the secret to life.

3 SPIRITUAL WARFARE TACTICS

Before this chapter unfolds, I would like to share that God gives me glimpses of supernatural events in the spiritual realm concerning what we fight against on a daily basis. Not as often, but definitely often enough He also shows me glimpses of the upcoming battles that we will face. Now, whether we like it or not, this war based on the scripture in the book of Revelation will come to pass. Some of us are friends with Jesus and know the truth in this battle, while some of us are friends with Jesus and refuse to face the reality of the battle that is to come. And also, there are still some of us that don't yet know the I AM. I have noticed in our current culture, be it church culture, or simply the western culture, that people are oblivious to these spiritual beings all around us. There is good and there is evil. That is it. No in between. There is enlightenment, and there is blindness that has either blessed or corrupted the human race. I realize that this topic being discussed can bring a sense of fear with it, however, I must reference to two important scriptures on this matter. The first reference is in 2 Timothy 1:7 (NKJV) ***For God has not given us a spirit of fear, but of power and of love and of a sound mind.***

This scripture rings true in talking about demons, end times, war, famine, disorder, disaster and chaos!

Fear is a demon that is sent to affect us and scare us into doubting or not trusting God. This spirit of fear has been assigned to solely infiltrate our peace; to penetrate the depths of our soul in a nasty way. I will elaborate on this demon in particular in an upcoming chapter. I just want to offer you a sense of love and peace from Jesus, the Prince of Peace, before delving in. This brings me to the next scripture to comfort you as you read on. Psalm 27:5 (NKJV) ***For in the time of trouble He shall hide me in His pavilion; in the secret place of His tabernacle He shall hide me; He shall set me high upon a rock.***

In the pure simplicity of the life I lead now, I can only imagine the way this scripture will remain true in the times to come. As we proceed, if at any point you find yourself afraid, simply say this and mean it; "In the name of Jesus Christ, Spirit of fear, I bind you. You may not influence me in anyway as I read this book! "

I was given a dream not long ago that involved persecutors of those that love Jesus. In the dream, as I stood in a line with other women who were to be tortured, faced with a team of demonic beings that were dressed as human soldiers, I was spared. How you ask? Well somehow, I was invisible to them. They passed right by me as if I didn't exist. The warning from God was explicitly portrayed however, because I had to watch each woman go through some serious torturous act. While I stood in line, I didn't know God was going to spare my life, so the feelings of terror and repentance, along with a great sadness were all present in my being. I do not wish this type of situation upon anyone. It truly was a horrifying thing to witness. Now coming out of the dream, I realize the meaning behind God's protection.

To be in the secret place of His tabernacle is where He will hide me. He will hide us there if we know Him. When we are presented with these disastrous situations, it will be too late to try and get to know Him, His presence and His word. We must prepare now to defeat the enemy that has come to conquer, but loses the final fight. We must do all that Christ asks of us now, as I believe it is all a preparation for the times that are inevitably coming. I like to say "Remember when God is working, so is the devil! Dress yourselves with the armor of God before he strikes, not after."

When put in a situation of death and life, none of us know what we will do until we're there, but let's just contemplate this hypothetically for moment. Are you yoga enthusiasts out there going to do a downward dog when a gun is pointed at you? Or are you occultists going to do some fancy ritual for your life to be spared while burning alive? That could be tricky. Or how about any atheist out there? Are you going to believe in anything greater than you, good or evil? Who will you turn to or call on when faced with death? I believe it will be in your innate nature to call on something bigger than you when faced with death. Now I assume you are an individual reading this book without anyone around, so I ask you to take a moment and deeply consider the ramifications of ignoring Jesus Christ's call for you. You, my friend, are His cherished masterpiece created in His very image. He died for you, and took every sin away for you. Oh, how He loves you! Dare I say that He is speaking to you now and the truth is touching your very soul. Embrace Him now!

God is always speaking. If we are walking in His Spirit we will hear Him. I don't care where we are, what we are doing or who we are around, He is talking. Part of the walk God has for me here on earth is going out into the darkness. He sends me to places that are covered with blankets of lust, greed, sadness, suicide, and perversion. I often find myself in bars, restaurants, clubs, and even strip clubs.

Just the other night, I knew God was planning some type of evening for me. My prayer during the day was very specific, yet nothing I would have come up with. I could feel He was stirring something in me and that I was going to be used to speak to someone. He gave me a name, and said he needs healing from losing a loved one. So I got up, got dressed and headed out. From the time I left my house, I prayed in tongues so that my prayers would be in perfect alignment with His will. Then He began to translate the tongues, allowing me to pray aloud in English. Following the first step of obedience leads to the next step of action. After this, I was invited to an event for the HBO show ***Ballers*** Season 2 Release Party in 2016. All was well. There were many familiar faces from TV and everything was going exactly as it should have been. Then after this event, my friend and I left to go to a club on South Beach. I thought nothing of it. This is a relatively normal thing that God does in my life. But I remained in His spirit the entire time.

I began to feel strange, I knew God's heart was breaking. Then as I sat in the VIP section with 20 bottles of Champagne surrounding me, as well as beautiful women, and many celebrities, I looked up out of habit and asked God what was wrong. With the sounds of hip hop music blasting in the background, the bass was so great the room shook with vibrations. I sought God. He opened my eyes at this very moment. I looked around to see hundreds of people lost. Demons surrounding them, causing them to thrust and sexually move on one another. Demons sat over people's eyes with their legs wrapped around their necks. Demons standing on their feet making them move, how and where they desired. Demons flying around the ceiling, waving the music frequencies to reach everyone's ears. Laughingly they flew. These sick, twisted, and vulgar beings were saturating the entire place. I had to stop and pray immediately to break all agreement with any of the demons attached to the music. Then after He showed me all of this, He said, "Remember Orlando."

Now, for those of you that don't know, a few weeks before this, on June 12, 2016, a gay club in Orlando was overtaken with terrorists. Many lost their lives that night. Many suffered fear, and pain that night. As I contemplated on what had transpired at that horrific event, He began to show me the hallways behind the walls that I could take to exit out of the back of the building I was currently in. As He was speaking to me, I of course thought about why He had sent me to a place that could possibly take my very life. But as I prayed He told me that this is how it was going to be. He will warn me when to leave a place! He will tell me when to leave, who to take, and how to get out. He loves me so much that He will tell me these things before they happen, as to protect me from this evil. I ask you, would I have known any of this had I not been walking in His Spirit? The answer is no. He is always talking so we should always be listening.

As the evening continued, one person really stood out. I think it was the fact that he had on a shirt with a symbol of Jesus on the pocket. I just smiled, thinking maybe someone else here was doing the same thing. However, lo and behold, by the end of the night, God led him straight to me. We began to have a discussion. He was a professional soccer player, and his friend had passed away about a year prior. This was the man that needed healing from the lost loved one! God loved him so much that He sent me to let him know God is here.

He taught me many lessons in one night, and as I share these stories with you, I pray that my testimonies lead you closer to Him. That evening, along with all of the other times that God uses me, are part of my purpose. They not only open my eyes to the things of the world that destroy people, but also, give glimpses of hope for those God is calling.

Let's move into a further understanding of this epic battle. In order for us to fight against the enemy in general, as well as in the end times, we are going to have to first understand that we are at war. Ephesians 6:12 (NLT) famous scripture used widely in Christian circles, churches and ministries, states the following:

> ***For we are not fighting against flesh-and-blood enemies, but against evil rulers and authorities of the unseen world, against mighty powers in this dark world, and against evil spirits in the heavenly places.***

Now, what does this really mean if we break it down? For we "war, fight, struggle," etc. We do not fight against people, animals, corporations, bosses, friends, spouses, government or anything made of flesh and blood, but against principalities. The definition of principality, according to Merriam-Webster Incorporated ©, is:

> The state, office, or authority of a prince; the position or responsibilities of a principal; the territory or jurisdiction of a prince: the country that gives title to a prince; an order of angels.

And in the ***Strong's Concordance*** Greek: 746, it defines principality as "Far above all principality, and power, and him, which is the head of all principality."

It is so important that we understand first what it is that we are warring against before we dive into battle. Just as God has a Kingdom that is placed in heaven. His fallen angel Lucifer, also has a kingdom. The meaning of the name Lucifer is described in Isaiah 14:12 as ***Day Star*** (ISV) or ***son of the morning*** (KJV) He was a heavenly angel that God created to worship Him. His place was in the very presence of God in Heaven's throne room. Just as God created the other angels and cherubims with love, Lucifer too was created ***as "the anointed cherub who covers;"*** Ezekiel 28:14 (NKJV).) According to God, as written in the scriptures, in Ezekiel 28:12 (NKJV) Lucifer was ***"the seal of perfection, full of wisdom and perfect in beauty."*** He was wise and beautiful. The reason I feel it necessary to point out who satan once was is to gain the proper perspective of the power he once had in the very presence of God, to who he became. Isaiah 14: 12-13 (NLT) gives us the best visual we need to grasp the importance of knowing the enemy we must fight. It states:

> ***"How you are fallen from heaven O shining star, son of the morning! You have been thrown down to the earth, you who destroyed the nations of the world. For you said to yourself, I will ascend to heaven and set my throne above God's stars. I will preside on the mountain of the gods far away in the north."***

I believe that after his fall from heaven, he decided to anchor his ship, land his turf, and establish his kingdom above the stars in the atmosphere. This is why the scripture I referred to earlier, Ephesians 6:12 (NIV), says that we are fighting ***against the powers of this dark world and against the spiritual forces of evil in the heavenly realms.*** For some, this brings up the question of how satan's kingdom can be in the heavenlies? I would like to address this by beginning with the scripture on the third heaven. In 2 Corinthians 12:1-10 (NKJV):

The Vision of Paradise

It is doubtless not profitable for me to boast. I will come to visions and revelations of the Lord: I know a man in Christ who fourteen years ago—whether in the body I do not know, or whether out of the body I do not know, God knows—such a one was caught up to the third heaven. And I know such a man—whether in the body or out of the body I do not know, God knows— how he was caught up into Paradise and heard inexpressible words, which it is not lawful for a man to utter. Of such a one I will boast; yet of myself I will not boast, except in my infirmities. For though I might desire to boast, I will not be a fool; for I will speak the truth. But I refrain, lest anyone should think of me above what he sees me to be or hears from me.

This clearly states that the third heaven is a utopia which leads me to my next question. If there is a third heaven, there must be a first and second heaven. If this is correct, then what are they like and why are they there? As I began to research this, and also asked God for supernatural insight, He gave me a revelatory notion about these heavens that are spoken of in the Bible. It is so important to have an understanding of partaking in the Kingdom of God on earth and having the mentality to understand how we, as the body of Christ, His very church, are to survive these times. It is also important for His Kingdom to be evident here on earth for those people that do not yet understand or have a relationship with Him. Hence making it equally as important to have the knowledge and tools on how to do so.

Sometimes it is difficult to differentiate between the reality of the world in which we live and the spiritual realm. It is in this world that our actual salvation or sin will lead to life or death. We must learn to look into the supernatural realm of God, instead of what is directly in front of us, to understand the realm of the heavenlies. A gift God gives is known as discernment of spirits. It is key to having a better understanding of these realms. This gift will also assist in the understanding of the beings that we must fight with the power of Christ.

On to the second heaven. What is it, and where is it? The Bible says in Deuteronomy 4:19 (NLT):

> ***And when you look up into the sky and see the sun, moon, and stars—all the forces of heaven—don't be seduced into worshiping them. The Lord your God gave them to all the peoples of the earth.***

As He warns us not to look up where the moon and stars are, He states not to be drawn away to worship and serve them. Who is He speaking of? There are many religions that have been around for centuries and longer that were drawn into the deceptive worship of the stars and the gods behind the stars. According to Wikipedia, it is called Astrolatry[3].

> Astrolatry is the worship of stars and other heavenly bodies as deities, or the association of deities with heavenly bodies. The most common instances of this are sun gods and moon gods in polytheistic systems worldwide. Also notable is the association of the planets with the deities in Babylonian, and hence in Greco-Roman religion, Mercury, Venus, Mars, Jupiter and Saturn. The term astro-theology is used in the context of 18th to 19th century scholarship aiming at the discovery of the original religion, particularly primitive monotheism. Unlike astrolatry, which usually implies polytheism, frowned upon as idolatrous by Christian authors since Eusebius, astrotheology is any 'religious system founded upon the observation of the heavens,' and in particular, may be monotheistic. Babylonian astronomy from early times associates stars with deities, but the heavens as the residence of an anthropomorphic pantheon, and later monotheistic God and his retinue of angels, is a later development, gradually replacing the notion of the pantheon residing or convening on the summit of high mountains.

The Bible states in Genesis 1:14 (KJV):

And God said, Let there be lights in the firmament of the heaven to divide the day from

the night; and let them be for signs, and for seasons, and for days, and years:

These signs were given to notate different times for us as the earth evolves. They were also used as a navigational compass. In Genesis 15:5 God told Abraham to look at the stars in remembrance of His promise to him. That's all Abraham had to do was look up at the many stars in the sky and he would remember that the seeds of the nation were to be his. The royal astrologers of the Babylonian court could not help to interpret the king's dreams. Why do you think this was so? Our great Father in heaven knew that people would see the power in the stars instead of using them for the purpose he wanted. He knew that they would begin to use forms of divination utilizing their power. If the second heaven is satan's lair, and Lucifer himself was referred to as a "falling star," I am inclined to think that there are other fallen demonic angels behind the secrets of theses stars. The Bible says that one-third of the angels from heaven followed him.

Divination is the practice of seeking out knowledge of the future or the unknown by supernatural means. I would urge any of you that consult astrology readings or any type of planet horoscopes to stop now. God forbade the children of Israel to worship or serve the "host of heaven." The problem with this is the same problem as other idol worship listed in the Bible. We cannot look to any other means besides Jesus, the Father Jehovah, and the Holy Spirit to know secrets of the future. It is not because they aren't capable of working, but rather a lack of trusting God's perfect plan and sovereign hand in our lives. Astrology can work. Psychics do know parts of the future. Tarot card readers can be accurate.

Principalities of evil, fallen angels, and demons all have knowledge of the supernatural realm. But when people operate through any name but Jesus, they are 100% getting their information from the demonic minions. They are taking orders from the higher ranked officials dwelling in the second heaven.

I realize you're probably thinking that the sweet little woman that reads your cards can't be affiliated with demons. Let me assure you that is exactly who she is consulting, and on your behalf! So it is not only the medium that uses herself or himself for this act, but because you are listening and willing to believe these words, you are forming an agreement in the supernatural realm with these demons. To broaden this picture in hopes that you will never again seek anything by means of foretelling your future, I would like you to take a moment and picture this. You are sitting with your trusted advisor, let's call her Nancy, and she tells you that Bob is going to propose in a year and that you will have one child, but you will also lose a child during this marriage. Also that you and Bob call it quits ten years into the marriage. Bob will find a younger more riveting women that steals his heart. Ok! Now it is here at this exact moment you begin to process these words in your mind. Either you are in disbelief and ask yourself why you came to see Nancy anyway, or you think it all sounds very possible, except that Bob would never cheat on you.

As your mind is attempting to wrap around all of this new information, there are plenty of demons whispering in your ears, pulling strings on your heart, and ultimately trying to get you to obsess over this new information. Why do they want you to obsess? Being tempted by something is not a sin. Getting angry is not a sin, but it is when we stay angry and allow ourselves to get enraged or develop resentment toward someone.

Obsessing on anything will lead to opening a new door to the demonic supernatural realm, allowing them to go from whispering in your ears, to influencing your life. I have included information in more detail in the last chapter on how we let demons in. God's love for us is so great that He warned us of these divinations. Do you think He is some cruel God that doesn't want you to know your future? Of course not. Rather, it is the exact opposite of that. He loves you so much He wants you to know the accurate, God breathed future for your life. He will tell you exactly what He wants you to know when He wants you to know it. Sometimes this is very different than what we want or think. If you are walking with Christ, then you know and accept that He knows best. There is only one way to get this type of information, and that is through my friend and all- knowing provider Jesus Christ of Nazareth. He may tell you directly through an angel or through a prophetic person, but He will tell you if you ask. If you don't believe what I am saying, ask Jesus to open your eyes to the spiritual realm around you next time you go to see good old Nancy. Then perhaps you will fully understand why God says this in Isaiah 47:13-14 (NLT):

> ***All the advice you receive has made you tired. Where are all your astrologers, those stargazers who make predictions each month? Let them stand up and save you from what the future holds. But they are like straw burning in a fire; they cannot save themselves from the flame. You will get no help from them at all; their hearth is no place to sit for warmth.***

So again here we are. When faced with death, will

any of these tools of horoscopes and atrology help you? It is written in His Word, and the answer is a big, fat, "**No**!"

I want to share the following story in hopes that it will help to save lives.

Once upon a time there was a girl who was full of love and life. She dreamed and wanted to know the plans for her life. She wanted to know all that God had for her. As she struggled in unknown territory with a man that was like none other she had met, she entered into a place of mystery. She had known that God had placed him in her life, but she couldn't wrap her mind around why things weren't going the way she thought they ought. So at the young age of 19, a fresh baby in Christ, she studied the Bible and went to church. She wrote songs of love and pain. She studied the religion and way of life that he practiced. She travelled, enjoying the world and what God had given her. She was sweet as honey, and walked like a gazelle; as in the poetry in Song of Solomon. She was an excellent woman in every way. Yet there seemed to be no answers for her. There seemed to be a huge disconnect in her theory of what she felt God had told her years prior.

So living in a place with many cultures from east to west, she heard much talk of New Age practitioners, Santeria, voodoo, Shamanism, psychics and many more. One day, she decided to inquire about such things. She didn't need to dig very deep because there were many people willing to steer her in the "right" direction.

Eventually, she found herself standing at the front door of a botanica. A botanica is a retail store that sells folk medicine, religious candles and statuary, amulets, and other products regarded as magical or as alternative medicine. They also carry oils, incense, perfumes, scented sprays (many of which are thought to have special properties) and various brand name health care products. Botanicas almost always feature a variety of products used in Roman Catholic religious practice such as rosary beads, holy water, and images of saints. Among the latter, the Virgin of Guadalupe and other devotional figures with a Latin American connection are especially well represented. The Catholic Church allows herbal medicine but prohibits magic and other religions. However, most botanica have products associated with other spiritual practices such as candomble, curanderismo, espiritismmo, macumba, santeria, voodoo, and hoodoo.

As she stood in front of this door, her heart was pumping with excitement and fear. Was this okay she asked herself. Were all these friends of hers guiding her into a new way of life that could answer all her prayers? She courageously walked in. There was a strange calm in the air. It was a heavy weighted atmosphere. It felt like she was walking through a thick cloud of invisible particles. As she looked around at all of the statues, candles, herbs, and strange artifacts, she noticed there was no one at the counter. What kind of store was this? Who should she speak to of her issues? When at last, a tall dark man slowly moved from a secret back room to the counter. His eyes were dark, his skin was wrinkled with a tinge of grey interweaved throughout the large pores on his face. His eyes were bloodshot with strings of red striking his pupils. With his strong Cuban accent, he offered her help. She felt strange about telling him any intimate details of her life, so she simply shared some small non-descriptive basics. He chuckled creepily at her story, reached down under his counter and handed her a small bag. He then gave her instructions on what to do with this strange little pouch that was tightly fastened in a small satchel.

As she left, she felt a strange breeze on her hair. It was unnerving. It put fear into the depths of her body. She got into her car and began to cry. She cried at the thought of needing anything besides God. She cried at the thought of all she had been taught and was now turning her back on. She got out of her car, threw the packet away and told herself that this would be the last time she would inquire of such things. Something about the whole experience felt wrong deep down inside of her. The feeling of conviction, the feelings of guilt and a depth of pain that began to surface when she entered that place were evident.

Days and weeks passed. She went on with her life the best way she knew how. But every few nights, she was reminded of this experience she had. She felt badly about it, but at the same time, contemplated each moment of her experience. As she did this, she thought of the calm in the air when she walked through the front door. It reminded her of God's calm. She thought of her hair being moved by some unseen force of wind, and it reminded her of God.

Week after week she contemplated this idea. With much thought, she decided that she was too quick to judge the situation accurately and decided to return to the store. With excitement, she scheduled a day that she could run some errands, and attempt this whole thing again. She pulled up to the parking lot and noticed there were few cars there. She parked, got out and walked up to the door, but it was locked. Closed! What should she do now? She was so ready to take his advice that day. She observed the sign, hoping to find a phone number, when a beautiful young woman coming from the mini mart next door approached. She said "Oh they are closed today. But if you're looking for some help, I have a guy." She couldn't believe it! Had God set this up for her to go somewhere else? The woman proceeded to share some stories about the man she thought she should see, so naturally, she took down all his information and left. She drove straight there wondering if it were possible that God had sent her to a new man; hopefully the right man, to help her.

As she pulled up, she confidently opened the front door. Observing all of the tools, oils, and statues, she noticed it was a bit different from the last place. There were some similarities for sure, but it was not quite the same. This disheveled, sweet looking chubby man stood at the counter waiting to greet her with a smile. He had a nice smile, smooth skin, and kind eyes. He had a striped button up shirt with one side hanging out and the other tucked in tightly with his big belly poking out. His socks were many colors and did not match his shirt or pants at all. He was a bit of a mess, but too adorable to ignore.

He asked how she needed help and then began to tell her things about her life that she hadn't shared with him. He was accurate in his words, and extremely kind in the delivery of such meaningful information. He said he was a Shaman. She didn't know much about this word, as she had only heard it once or twice before in her lifetime. He invited her to sit with him and discuss her situation; upon which he offered her a free tarot card reading. Now she had never had a card reading, and didn't know much about it except that it could foretell her future. So she graciously accepted the offer.

He began to tell her of her past, present, and future. The things he said were so accurate that there seemed to be a burst of an emotional awakening! After this, he said he wanted to see her again to work out the rest. He asked if he could put his hands on her head and when he did, he said some type of prayer over her. This prayer was none like she had ever heard. It was exhilarating! He assured her that from that moment on she would feel like a million bucks and boy was he right! She got in her car, pumped gas, and went to the grocery store, all with this feeling of beauty and power. She began to notice changes in her personal life as well. She held a power that she had never felt before with her boyfriend, and it was exactly what she had wanted. It felt like home to her. It felt like she was finally visible to those she loved. But about two weeks later, it was all gone. It seemed she was back where she had begun. Of course she decided to go back to the shaman. Why wouldn't she? He made her feel like the woman God had designed her to be!

She began seeing him regularly. At least once a month she went to him. Before she could even tell him what was happening in her life, he would tell her. He opened her eyes to so much because he could see what was really going on. It was as if everything you ever wanted to know about your life was sitting in one man's head. He also told her of gifts that she had. He told her that she too can see in the future, and that it had happened to her before. She agreed with him and told him that Jesus tells her things. He just nodded his head and offered her classes free of charge to learn how to use her powers from God. About a week before these classes were to begin, something happened. Something changed.

She would be in a deep sleep and wake up unable to move her body. As she would lay in fear, she was paralyzed by some great force that would torment her for spans of time throughout each night. She was afraid to walk down the hall to her bedroom in the dark. She was seeing things in her room that reminded her of college years. "That's it!" She exclaimed. This was the same fear, and the same shadows she had seen years before when God had activated her gifts to see demons and angels. Only at this time, she saw only demons. Great in size and great in power. They would sit in her room and stare at her. They would torment her as she slept. They would tell her things that were the total opposite of what God had told her years before. What had she done? How could this have happened? She cried out in fear. She cried and cried and cried. She asked God what these horrible things were and why she trembled with fear daily. To her surprise, she heard nothing. She remained in fear, not knowing how to fix it.

Postponing the classes, it came time for a trip home. She had planned to go see her family where she grew up and was overly nervous for the flight. When she got to the airport she felt only anxiety. She felt anxiety so intensely that it grew into a full blown attack while the plane took off. Her heart felt like it was pumping out of her chest; she could hear a small voice that whispered in her ear that she was going to die. It said she couldn't leave Miami or she would die. Fearing the worst for herself she breathed deeply and the anxiety settled some for the rest of the flight. When she arrived and was safe with her family, she felt very unsettled. The ceiling fans were making her dizzy. She thought she was going to faint. There were shadows following her. There was a deep emotional battle going on inside of her heart. And then she looked down and it seemed her stomach had grown. What is this? Why had her stomach been flat 2 days prior, but now it was swollen and distorted? She began to cry in anguish, wondering if she was going to die.

She pleaded with her sister to take her to the

emergency room as she knew it was the end of her life. Her sister didn't understand what was wrong. She had only known her to be a calm, laid back, put together girl. What was happening here? She rushed her to the ER where the doctors performed test after test. Pregnancy tests, bladder infection tests, thyroid tests, CAT scans checking organs, and blood tests to check levels. She thought for sure this was the time her life was coming to an end. As she laid in the hospital bed shaking uncontrollably, her sister told her that she was going to be alright. She could only find one form of peace. All shaking would stop and all fear would leave, but only when she would close her eyes and picture Jesus floating above her breathing into her mouth. Every time she would stop and do this, she was in complete and utter peace. But when she would open her eyes, back to the natural world. She would return to shaking and fear.

The doctors came in and told her that nothing at all was medically wrong with her. They said it must be some weight gain. Her sister laughed and said, "weight gain in 2 days? How is that possible? She looked about fifteen pounds lighter two days ago!" They assured everyone that nothing medically seemed to be wrong. She silently went through the motions of the day, remembering how deeply touched she was when Jesus had breathed into her. The rest of the trip was repeated anxiety attacks and constant thoughts of death and destruction. She would lay in bed and hold herself back from making her mom or sister take her back to the emergency room. There were momentary glimpses of peace when Jesus would show up and breathe into her mouth. But it was all too much for her. She had hit her limit. Jesus was now all she had to combat this fear of death and torment.

When she returned home, she had decided that it

was the Shaman man that had affected her. It had to be. It was the only thing different she had done. This is when God explained to her what she had done. The use of the beautiful young woman to direct her to the Shaman. He used demons that he had placed over her when he would say his prayers and do his rituals was the problem. She had come into agreement with the satanic realm. He had enticed her and she had allowed satan himself to torment her. She had signed on the dotted line next to satan and didn't even know she had done it. But as it turned out, she found herself back in the arms of Jesus.

It was not an easy process to return back into His arms, as she had to learn how to break all agreement, and all curses that were placed upon her life. But by the grace of God, she found her way in to rest, and began to know her path in His perfect timing. It was at that moment that God, the Father of Abraham, Isaac, and Jacob spoke to her.

I pray that through this story, which is actually my testimony of what happened personally to me, that you have gained an understanding of how this demonic force worms its way into a precious life. Seemingly innocent, he will do all he can to get you. He will not stop until he is stopped by the power that only Jesus can give you.

So when discussing the war we are in, knowingly or not, there is a strategy for both good and evil. God is talking about being vigilant; not to worship the powers that dwell in this very kingdom. At the end of the scripture I spoke on before the story, He refers to heaven as "whole heaven." If there is a whole pizza it must be broken down into pieces to eat. In the same way, heaven is broken into pieces, first heaven, second heaven, and third heaven. They are definitely not all the same heaven, or the heaven we all think of when hearing the word. There is a new perspective, a biblical perspective, on these different places, although scholars could not find anywhere in the Bible where He refers to this Kingdom as the "second heaven" in Genesis 1: 6-8 (NLT)

> ***Then God said, "Let there be a space between the waters, to separate the waters of the heavens from the waters of the earth." And that is what happened. God made this space to separate the waters of the earth from the waters of the heavens. God called the space "sky."***

Here He refers to heaven as heavens, an obviously a plural word meaning more than one. The emphasis that I am making here isn't about the specifics of how many heavens there are, rather, where they are and what they are made of. We must know our battle field. We must understand the environment, conditions, and terrain of the land! The following excerpt captures some of the warfare conditions during World War I that closely parallels the spiritual warfare we face on a daily basis. The diary of Colonel Joseph Hyde Pratt, "What were the living conditions in Trench Warfare"[4]

> The weather confined in World War I caused many soldiers to suffer severe diseases like Trench Foot. During the War, the grass and trees had been killed due to constant bombardment in the area. The earth was transformed into mud and slush from all the rain. This was in perfect condition for Trench Foot disease to occur. The weather affected the WWI soldiers by continuous dampness that was created by a mixture of defoliation and precipitation.

The damp conditions caused the injuries to become more infected as they didn't have a dry environment to heal in. During winter, most of the soldiers suffered due to frost bite and lack of warmth. However, in contrast to that, summer was completely different and many soldiers became dehydrated.

I give this example to show that when in war, the conditions of the environment are instrumental to the outcome being successful. Equally as important, we must also look at the game plan of the enemy. Let us take a look at the attack on Pearl Harbor (Wikipedia)[5]:

> The attack on Pearl Harbor was a surprise military strike conducted by the Imperial Japanese Navy against the United States naval base at Pearl Harbor, Hawaii, on the morning of December 7, 1941 (December 8 in Japan.) The attack led to the United States' entry into World War II. Japan intended the attack as a preventive action to keep the U.S. Pacific Fleet from interfering with military actions the Empire of Japan planned in Southeast Asia against overseas territories of the United Kingdom, the Netherlands, and the United States. There were simultaneous Japanese attacks on the U.S held Philippines and on the British Empire in Malaya, Singapore, and Hong Kong. The attack came as a profound shock to the American people and led directly to the American entry into World War II in both the Pacific and European theaters.

> There were a total of 2,403 American casualties, including 68 civilians, and 1178 military and civilians wounded.[6]

I am attempting to show you here how wars are dangerous and also how important it is to be well prepared. We must, as Christ followers, also be well prepared for a time in which no one knows the exact time. I am referring here to what Jesus said in Matthew 24:36 (NLT):

> ***"However, no one knows the day or hour when these things will happen, not even the angels in heaven or the Son himself. Only the Father knows."***

Because of this scripture, and others I haven't mentioned yet, we must prepare ourselves for these times that are coming. As days, months, and years pass, what we need to realize is that every day is a battle. You may thinking that what I'm saying sounds a bit dramatic, but I urge you to take heart. Every prayer, every desire, every need, every moment, there is a Lion waiting to devour you. He waits for perfect moments throughout a day to attack us and our ministries, our families, our purpose, our relationships and much more.

Let us get to know our enemy a bit shall we! 1 Peter 5:8 (NIV) says ***Be alert and of sober mind. Your enemy the devil prowls around like a roaring lion looking for someone to devour.***

It is clear in this text that satan doesn't multitask with an array of things to do each day, or make monumental decisions with hopes of becoming a rocket scientist some day. He has one goal. He has one mission.

He has one purpose. He wants to destroy all of God's people and God's kingdom. His desire is for all humanity to suffer and hate, but even more so, Christians. Why? Well as Christ-followers one of our main missions is to save souls through Christ for the Kingdom of God for His glory. So because of the battle satan is having with God, and the two opposite purposes of Christians and the devil being directly on the far end of the spectrum, it is a direct hit to those who have Christ dwelling within them. This is WAR!!

In Ephesians 6:12 (NKJV), God says we:

> ***wrestle . . . against principalities, against powers, against the rulers of the darkness of this age, and against spiritual hosts of darkness in the heavenly places.***

In I Peter 5:8 b (NLT), He compares satan to a ***roaring lion, looking for someone to devour.*** This gets my imagination going. Just picture a lion in the jungle with an insatiable appetite, a bottomless pit, walking slowly but steadfastly through the brush pouncing on anything breathing, in an attempt to fulfill his never ending appetite. Does this picture make you look behind your shoulder a bit? It most certainly should! But my point here is that satan is an invisible force with an invisible army, although he does have ways of operating in the physical realm. Let's look at the following scriptures:

> ***Then the Lord God said to the serpent, "Because you have done this, you are cursed more than all the animals, domestic and wild. You will crawl on our belly, groveling in the dust as long as you***

live."
Genesis 3:14 (NLT).

But He [Jesus] turned and said to Peter, "Get behind Me, satan! You are an offense to Me, for you are not mindful of the things of God, but the things of men."
Matthew 16:23 (NKJV).

In this narrative, Jesus was speaking to his disciples, giving them a lesson while also was speaking prophetically about His walk on earth. Peter was having trouble embracing all that Jesus was telling him and spoke out to Him. Why would He look at His disciple and speak to satan? The reason is because satan uses us. He can speak through us, move through us, and influence us in many ways. This scripture clearly shows that. Understand that part of this journey is Jesus rebuking and delivering us from satan and his demons. Also, may I point out here that Peter was a Christ-follower. So does this mean that Christians too can be affected by demons and satan? Yes! In the following chapters I will go more in depth on this scriptural principle. The next Bible verse depicting this principle is Acts 5:3 (NKJV) it states:

But Peter said, "Ananias, why has satan filled your heart to lie to the Holy Spirit and keep back part of the price of the land for yourself?"

I believe that God shows us many times in the Bible that satan is definitely active in the spirit realm, and also that he can influence, as well as enter, humans and animals. The Bible says, ***Then satan entered Judas,***

surnamed Iscariot, who was numbered among the twelve. Luke 22:3 (NKJV).

I would say this is pretty self- explanatory. So what can we do to prevent satan from influencing us, or worse case entering us? Be ready to attack before he does. Just as the military uses tactics to win war, so can we. I strongly feel that the fight we walk out today, is the preparation for the end times when the going will get tough. Because we do not know the time, although some scholars feel we will have three and a half years after the peace treaty in Israel is signed, we are on a steady downslide to the end. Biblical prophecy, worldly and government current standing, and even many recent natural disasters, all point to the end times coming our way. Would God want us to be prepared for this? And if so, how does He want us to prepare?

Because it is a spiritual battle, which I pray has been made evident thus far, we must prepare spiritually. When the military train for war, they ready their physical bodies, mental strengths, plans of attack, strategies, and usually have a plan B if plan A doesn't go as hoped. These are the same training tactics we will use to prepare for our King coming to get us, and also living victoriously as Christ-followers until this day comes.

The preparation for fighting in the spirit realm is oddly simple if you discover and apply the how-to's of how God intends for us to stay in a state of readiness. I will give a couple of examples so that you can imagine how to begin to apply this in your own life.

Before I go anywhere I spend time in worship and prayer. Then I continue to pray in my car. I pray for the Holy Spirit to be present all around me and within me in order to do God's work while I'm out. It doesn't matter if I'm headed to dinner, a bar, a club, or a church crusade, I always ask for God to use me as a vessel in order for His will to be done in my life. As I am writing this book, I am also still living life. This leads me to a quick story of what happened to me just the other night because I did not pray for protection or ask to be used. I was hurrying to get ready to go for dinner with some friends while my daughter slept. I didn't want to wake her so I played my worship music quietly while doing my hair. This in itself became a distraction from my normal routine because I could barely hear the music to engage with His Holy Spirit. This led to misdirected thoughts such as; I'll never be ready on time, my hair looks ridiculous, is this red lipstick too red? Will my daughter have a nightmare? Should I go at all or just stay home to pray. As all of these unnecessary thoughts were racing through my head, my dearly loved Mother called to chat. I answered but told her I couldn't really talk because I was headed out and getting ready. She then said it would be okay for me to call her when I was on my way. I agreed and we hung up. Now, little did I know that my usual thirty minute car ride of worship, praise, and discerning direction for my evening would be so missed and also could have spared me from the negative happenstances that occurred. Although I thought of hanging up and praying several times, I spent the whole ride discussing my Mom's recent trip to Hawaii. We finally hung up the phone as I was parking my car. I fixed my lipstick and headed into the restaurant.

Within the first fifteen minutes of being there, someone ordered an incredibly flamboyant cocktail that just happened to use dry ice as an ice cube. I looked in wonderment at the pretty red drink that was smoking up the bar with glistening crystals of ice. A friend thought it would be a good idea to pour some of the dry ice on the glossy finished bar to watch it separate and spread over the bar like a film of crystals cascading over the edge. It was beautiful, and exciting! I could feel the cold air blowing over my legs. Had it all stopped there, it would have been a perfect little experience for me, but the same friend that threw it on the bar decided to throw it on my left leg. I realized quickly that yes, it was cold, but even more so, it was burning my leg! I sat quietly rubbing my jeans hoping that the sensation would soon pass. It did not. I then decided Jesus could heal it quickly, so I went to the restroom to pray. This is also something I do often when I'm out to remain in the Holy Spirit while surrounded by darkness. Yes, it is a dark world out there. At any rate, while in my stall, I raised my hand searching for the Holy Spirit's presence, and a healing anointing to fall upon me. I felt very, very little of it. I asked God why I was struggling to feel Him, when He quickly replied that this place had many idols and relics that angered God. So I then pled the blood of Christ over me, put on the full armor of God, and tried again. By His faithful love, He showed up and began to heal my leg. The redness of the burn slowly dissipated, but the pain stayed strong. I spent about fifteen minutes praying in that bathroom stall that evening, discerning what exactly needed healing. I had to speak to the burn itself, to the nerve endings that were injured, and to the pain. God showed me through this experience how very important it is to always be protected by the sword of the spirit and the shield of faith. Without this divine tool, we have more of a chance to be harmed by the enemy who dwells in the spirit realm. This was not the flesh at work, it was satan simply taking advantage of the fact that I didn't take time to pray and protect myself before leaving. Does this make any of you think about the importance of praying before you go anywhere or do anything? I was considering wearing a skirt that evening. Can you imagine the damage to my leg had I done so? This is not to be taken lightly. The degree at which satan will attack us is not necessarily the important part of this story, rather, that satan will indeed attack! He does not sleep, he does not blink, but he is rendered powerless when we have the hedge of protection of God the Father around us.

The next day as I looked down at my beautifully, perfectly healed leg, I was in awe over God's complete healing! I began to ask Him questions. Why do we have to constantly pray for protection if we are God's child? Why can't we just have a constant bubble around us that fights satan? As I sought and prayed on the matter He began to talk to me more about the flesh and the soul, and how to warfare against both.

The first scripture that I was led to was Romans 13:12-14 (NASB):

> ***The night is almost gone, and the day is near Therefore let us lay aside the deeds of darkness and put on the armor of light. Let us behave properly as in the day, not in carousing and drunkenness, not in sexual promiscuity and sensuality, not in strife and jealousy. But put on the Lord Jesus Christ, and make no provision for the flesh in regard to its lusts.***

Children are afraid of the dark for a reason. Satan loves to move at night. It is known that around 3 AM or 3:15 AM, which some call the witching hour, is an inversion of the time that Christ died on Calvary. Leave it to satan to pervert something holy. Also, most of these sins I am referring to in this scripture have a tendency to occur more in the evening time than in the daytime. I stress the phrase "occur more" because trust me when I say. It also happens in the daytime, as I have seen firsthand; however, I would say that it is more likely in the evening. God knew this, of course. Sometimes He is speaking in a literal sense, where as other times, He is speaking in a symbolic sense of good verses evil; God verses the devil. Sin itself is in every individual that exists on this great earth, but the key here is more about what doors they have opened for satan to go gallivanting around in their lives. I could go on for days about these particular sins mentioned in the above quote, but this book is not focusing on sin, rather on fighting and defeating satan in the spirit realm. So onward we push!

Notice the words, ***"But put on the Lord Jesus Christ, and make no provisions for the flesh in regard to its lust."*** Here Paul is explaining the importance of literally wearing Jesus! Put Him on like a jacket, pants, shoes, hat, and sunglasses! This scripture is a definitive example of what I forgot to do that night in the car, or rather, chose not to do. When I am preparing for an evening out, as I pray aloud putting actual breath to scripture, I am surrounding myself with a special covering over my life. John 1:4 (NLT) says:

The Word gave life to everything that was created, and his life brought light to everyone.

Because I am righteous in God's eyes and wear my robe well, when I speak, my words too, give life to everything that is created. So as I speak protection of Christ's blood over me, His blood is then poured over me from the top of my head to the souls of my feet. In the spirit realm this is a very literal thing. Just because we cannot see His blood on us, does not mean it isn't there. In the same way, when we put on the full armor of God we are literally putting on Christ as Paul instructs us to do. So take heed to these words and protect yourselves, first with His blood, and then with the whole armor of God.

> *Therefore put on the full armor of God, so that when the day of evil comes, you may be able to stand your ground, and after you have done everything, to stand. Stand firm then, with the belt of truth buckled around your waist, with the breastplate of righteousness in place, and with your feet fitted with the readiness that comes from the gospel of peace. In addition to all this, take up the shield of faith, with which you can extinguish all the flaming arrows of the evil one. Take the helmet of salvation and the sword of the Spirit, which is the word of God. And pray in the Spirit on all occasions with all kinds of prayers and requests. With this in mind, be alert and always keep on praying for all the Lord's people.*
> Ephesians 6:13-18 (NIV).

I remember a time when I was hanging out with a few friends and they had invited a friend over that was a psychic. She said there was something different about me. She said I had a weird bubble of red and gold that surrounded me. Makes sense doesn't it? I was protected from any demons because of my Holy covering. This is real. This is more real than the things we do daily on the earthly realm.

I once asked God, while in a deep moment of intercession for someone very dear to me, why things can look so drastically different on earth than they do in the spirit realm. Earlier that day I was awakened by an extremely vivid dream. I was so overwhelmed by it that I had to look deeper. I had to pray harder for just a glimpse of what God was trying to tell me. I knew it was a dream of truth and instruction of a message from Him. How did I know such a thing for sure? The night before I decided to do some warfare to fight whatever had stopped me from dreaming or remembering my dreams the week previous. I spoke to all ungodly spirits that were in my home, around me or influencing me in any way. I spoke with the authority that I knew was given to me through Jesus. I commanded it go and then I gave Jesus permission to enter my dreams and to fight anything that was hindering me from having intimacy with Christ while I slept. Lo and behold I woke with this in depth, very complex dream. My search began from there. In this dream, It showed me a deep love that someone had for me. A love so deep, that there was a poem written on a glass case of rose pedals, giving me instruction of how this love was to last forever. This dream showed God's perspective of where this love was in the present and what I needed to proclaim over my life, finally ending with the future outcome of our joint ministry and purpose here on earth. I thought it was the most amazing thing that God loved me so much He confirmed the deep feelings I had for this person. I thought it was intriguing that my dream and the accuracy of it was so clear, but that on earth it was nothing like this. I began to ponder why the earthly realm is so very different from the spirit realm. I started to wonder just how many people would be more at peace and trusting God more if they knew His perspective. It started to perplex me on levels I had not yet experienced in my walk with Christ. I understood that the two realms were very different of course. I mean, after all, I could see demons and angels. I could get specific information about people that would set them free from pain and bondage. I laid hands on people and watched God heal them. I wrote songs as oil freely fell on my hands straight from heaven. I had a pretty good understanding of this spirit realm, or so I thought. But this dream forced me to look deeper, ask more questions, and pray more uninhibitedly. I needed to know why God spoke so clearly through a dream but it was not reflected in what I see in my every day life. This is where it is helpful to grasp that our beings are not just flesh.

Because we are made with a soul and spirit, as well as flesh, we cannot just look at the flesh outcomes. I like to look at it this way. Our flesh is affiliated with the earthly realm and everyday struggles or blessings, while our spirit is existing with Jesus in a place of no time and tangibility on the earthly realm. In a place of no time and the sovereign omnipotence of God, one can only imagine that it will look a lot different than this place. Although there are many lovely things about our world, there are equally as many saddening and unfortunate manifestations in our world. It can be depressing and overwhelming to think about sometimes, but the key is in knowing the Lord. If we know Christ, we can spend the majority of our time in the realm of truth that offers hope. This place is the truth. This place, dwelling with Jesus, if done on a regular basis will change your life. You will begin to see a different reality and perception of your problems than you ever have before. These things are so necessary for the end times. If we cannot see the hope in Jesus Christ's triumph in the defeat of satan and making all things new in the New Jerusalem, it will be difficult for us to partner with Him to achieve the goal. I did however find that there is a process to learning this lesson as well. ***Create in me a clean heart, O God, and renew a steadfast spirit within me.*** Psalm 51:10 (KJV).

It is important to understand that this scripture is teaching us not only how to pray, but also that God must create a clean heart. Not just purify or disinfect, but to literally create a new heart. According to ***Strong's Concordance*** (H1254), create, or *bará*, first used in Genesis 1:1, *bará* always involves God "to create, shape, form . . . of something new."

There are a few reasons I'm pushing this point. The first is to know that God must *bará* in us a clean heart to fully embrace this other world that exists. Otherwise when we enter it, it can become a dangerous thing for our very well being. When we are given a certain broadened divine perspective, our hearts must be new and also our spirits must be steadfast. According to ***Strong's Concordance*** (H539), the word faithful, or *'aman,* has been translated as "believe, assurance, faithful, sure, established, trust, verified, steadfast, continuance, . . . [and] trusty." This gives us a more in-depth understanding of the scripture and why it is important to ask God for this. You may be wondering what any of this has to do with things being different in the spirit realm, verses here on earth. In order to fathom the unfathomable, our hearts must be created clean, and our spirit must be faithful and loyal and completely adhered to God's spirit. If not will not only miss the mark, but may enter dangerous territory that we don't yet have the authority to enter. So, with the intention of our hearts being purified and faithful to God, He shows us the power behind these Rhema words in our dreams. When He speaks to us of things that aren't coinciding with that which we see here all around us, it is sometimes for instruction, sometimes for intercession, sometimes to show us the future and sometimes for us to speak forth the future of that which is His divine will.

Let me share with you a bit on the "seer" gift that God has blessed me with. There are many scriptures that talk about the seer gift, but today I want to refer to 1 Samuel 9: 9 (KJV):

> ***(Beforetime in Israel when man went enquire of God, thus he spake. Come, and let us go to the seer; for he that is now called a prophet was beforetime called a seer.)***

I am definitely not calling myself a prophet, however, if a seer has visions and sees in the supernatural realm, then that is what I am. To simplify this, I will say that God allows me to see angels and demons daily. I definitely see demons more often than angels however. I don't yet fully know why that is. Perhaps satan thinks he can intimidate me with demon. I have noticed, depending on where I am geographically, that these things can look different. When I go to certain places in Miami, I see demons flying in the sky. All over the place! They are everywhere, saturating the sky with dark snake like shadows that zoom and nose dive down to land. Also diving straight onto people. I sometimes see them flying in circles around me, and at times they land on my skin and moved about like creepy little snakes. It is at that moment that I command them to leave and they must! Then there are times when I notice that my mind isn't quite right or I am having impure thoughts that would sadden God, or I am overall just feeling far away from my best friend Jesus. It is at this time when I take a moment to ask God what is going on. More times than not, I see the demon shadows appear on my body or very close to my person. This is when God instructs me to do a deliverance prayer, at which time the nasty culprit that is causing the feeling of separation from Christ disperses from me and back out into the world or where ever God decides they should go.

There is a great difference between the demons that I see flying around actively tormenting people, and the very big principalities conducting and leading their direction of ambush. Having this gift allows me to help others. It allows a strategy of foreknowing that which plagues people. Jesus removes it and ultimately brings their relationship with God to the next level. I have also found it helpful when struggling with certain problems in life, to consult with God on satan's strategy on the particular situation. He without a doubt shows me, or tells me one way or another how to defeat that which satan thinks he will win. This is why the secret to winning the war is hearing the voice of God. We see through the eyes of Jesus. We have to have access to these hidden realms, otherwise, we will be defeated based on simply being born into sin. But if we look deeper, our own sin propels a consequence. Each thing we have done against God, willingly and knowingly, or unwillingly and unknowingly, reaps a judgment. Galatians 6:7-8 (ESV) touches upon this notion:

> ***Do not be deceived: God is not mocked, for whatever one sows, that will he also reap. For the one who sows to his own flesh will from the flesh reap corruption, but the one who sows to the Spirit will from the Spirit reap eternal life.***

And then in Romans 14:10-12 (ESV) it states the following:

> ***Why do you pass judgment on your brother? Or you, why do you despise your brother? For we will all stand before the judgment seat of God; for it is written "As I live, says the Lord, every knee shall bow to me, and every tongue shall confess to God." So then each of us will give an account of himself to God.***

I want you to understand that I am pointing out that the things of our past hold an accountability to our future. Once we have committed our lives to Christ, we've been cleansed of all our sins. We deserve God's judgment because we all break His laws, however, Jesus took every sin from us. He took every infirmity, every curse, and every thing that we could ever do, away. Now it rests upon Christ. Thankfully so because we would all be in big trouble otherwise. I feel that there were many moments when God showed me how a past sin affected my life in a negative way. Recently He showed me how a sin I committed sixteen years ago became a curse in my life. I was not aware of this until sixteen years later when He revealed this truth to me. Without going into specifics, I went through the appropriate steps that He showed me in order to break this curse. I noticed a sense of freedom immediately. I also noticed it in my life everywhere else from that point on. This whole experience intrigued me. I thought to myself that if God had revealed , at this moment in my life, the significance of this sin from years back. What else had I done! So I went into prayer before I slept asking God that if there are any other curses or past sins that are holding me back in any way, would He reveal them to me in my sleep. Then I gave only Jesus Christ of Nazareth permission to enter my dreams and sarturate my whole home in His blood. I do this so that demons have no legal way of entering my dreams or my house. It is a nightly routine for me and my family. So what do you know! The next morning I woke from a dream that concerned my past, a particular person, and a particular place. Was this a coincidence? Of course not. I asked, and He told. It's funny how many people don't ask. He is our best friend if you let Him be. As Matthew 7: 7-11 perfectly states in the Amplified Bible version:

> ***"Ask and keep on asking and it will be given to you; seek and keep on seeking and you will find; knock and keep on knocking and the door will be opened to you. For everyone who keeps on asking receives, and he who keeps on seeking finds, and to him who keeps on knocking, it will be opened. Or what man is there among you who, if his son asks for bread, will instead give him a stone? Or if he asks for a fish, will instead give him a snake? If you then (sinful by nature) as you are, know how to give good and advantageous gifts to your children, how much more will your Father who is in heaven [perfect as He is] give what is good and advantageous to those who keep asking Him."***

Now there is another side to this coin. God loves us so much that He will answer our prayers, however, in accordance with His will. This is why the refinement of our souls and the cleansing of our hearts is of utmost importance. In James 4:3 (NIV) it states ***When you ask, you do not receive, because you ask with wrong motives, that you may spend what you get on your pleasures.*** God must come first. God's Kingdom, in its entirety, must come first. God's desires and will, must come first. This isn't an easy thing to accept for a lot of people. It actually took me over half of my walk with Christ to get to this point whole heartedly. To surrender all to God with no hindrances is one of the most difficult challenges to walking in His spirit. Surrendering all is a daily choice that must start with humility. It is a challenge for many. But be encouraged; the closer you get to Him, the more demons that He removes, the more healing he ministers to your soul, the more you will want all He wants. So start with getting to know Him and He will take it from there.

These are but a few tactics that God has shown me to overcome satan. Now this is hour to hour, day to day, week to week, and year to year. Again I feel strongly that it is all preparation for what is to come. Without these teachings He gives me on a daily basis, I would never be ready for the times to come. When the darkness is so great and so horrifying there will be nowhere to turn. I already know I will not only be safe, but I will be used as well. How about you?

4 GOD THE CREATOR

God, as the creator of the world and of mankind, is the Alpha and the Omega. He is the first and the last. He is the beginning and the end. Our spirits are eternal with all the power of God. Our spirits dwelt with Him before we were sent into our mother's womb. When our spirits were put into our mother's womb to become life, it was to mirror that of Christ. This is because He too was there with us before our human bodies were put on earth. He was there! His Holy Spirit that was not yet born into human form was there. He hovered over all and this is why all things are possible through Christ. If everything was created by Him, then it is obvious that He has power over all of His creations. He has the last word on everything, no matter what. No man, no circumstance, and no evil can stop or hinder that which God speaks. You may ask yourself if this is true, then why would God allow so many things to happen. Understand that He does not cause anything bad. Satan is alive and kicking. Because God knows all and has the last word, then He most assuredly knows what we will do and how we will do it. It is so important to understand that our faith and our understanding of our new birthrights in Christ, and authority within these rights is only of benefit to us when we exercise this place of status. It's like having a cold bowl of rice and a microwave sitting in front of you. If you don't put the bowl in the microwave, hit the time frame you want, and click the start button, then you simply have a cold bowl of rice. In front of you sits everything you need to have a deliciously warm bowl of rice, yet it stays cold because you won't utilize the microwave. That is one of the biggest reasons that people of God get caught up in life rather than God's Kingdom, They either won't utilize the power God intentionally gave them, or the don't know how. If it is the first reason, then it is simply laziness, and if it is the latter, it is lack of knowledge. Either way it is a sin that we must repent for, and do what is right. When we cast out demons that cause these sins, a space is then allotted to the Holy Spirit to move freely in our spiritual lives. However we must give Holy Spirit permission to permeate our souls. ***"I will put My Spirit within you and cause you to walk in My statutes, and you will be careful to observe My ordinances."*** Ezekiel 36:27 (NASB). How have you been avoiding God's call on your life? I say with confidence that He is undoubtedly calling you. He is assuredly speaking to you. The question is, are you listening? He gave us His authority to call forth to create, and to speak that which is not into that which is; hence making all things possible through Christ. Jesus was always with God, but He wasn't sent in human form to die for us until later. However, because the time that we know as time is different from God and time, we understand that Jesus was with Him, was Him, was the word. He was born, died on the cross, and was resurrected all before we even read "In the beginning." I want to focus more on our understanding of God the Creator, to bring this point home.

We too, are a living form of God. This is why the more Christ-like Jesus makes us, the more miracles and unity with the creator are possible. Angels and demons are a supernatural creation just as we are, however, they dwell on a different dimension, or more simply put, at a different frequency, when measuring energy levels. They are not human, never have been, never will be, so their very existence is on a different level than ours. The more we operate on these levels, or allow God's gifting to manifest, the more Godly power we are able to possess. This is because His Spirit is fulfilling us on that frequency. I am referring to this space as frequency, not to encourage any new age phenomena, rather, to give a more scientific depiction of what God does in the supernatural realm. The deeper we search in His Spirit, the more translucent our physicality becomes. We become more energy than matter. We gain a "supernatural wisdom" that can override any obstacle or feeling involved with our man (flesh), because we are directly connected to the Holy Spirit which not only created us, but is teaching us through our spirit man how to become more like Him. By energy, I mean the same Spirit that breathed my spirit into existence. It urpasses all chromosomal momentum becoming much more present than that of my flesh. There are times when I am so enmeshed in the Presence of God that my body doesn't feel like a body at all. It feels like it could float off at any moment if God so desired. It tingles with a constant flow of His electricity surging through my veins. This space that I am speaking of is very special, yet very difficult to articulate. I do believe that the reason this happens is that it is a time of intimacy with the Creator. This is something all human beings have at their fingertips to experience! Are you going to hit the start button and utilize that which God offers?

Now, because of our flesh and our world being held

hostage by satan, it isn't possible to remain in this state forever, but then again, that's what we have to look forward to when we go to heaven. The purpose of this is for all to see His glory, to fear and love Him at exactly the right moment in time, therefore allowing Him to manifest into a supernatural anomaly for all to share. In the physical realm the pillow on which we lay our heads at night is not really a pillow, or even really there. Your brain tells you that it is there, it is real, and it is for comfort, but if we were to enter the spirit realm, the realm where there is no matter, no time, and no pillows. It is only energy and different frequencies. We can only fully understand this principal by spending time in His presence while becoming completely fulfilled with His Spirit. Let us be transfused with the Spirit of, in order to become like Him. This will allow supernatural wisdom, supernatural acceptance of money, supernatural understanding of time, and supernatural knowledge of your very purpose while here on earth. This will allow things to move from the supernatural realm to the the earthly realm.

When I see In the Spirit, the air, the sky, the wind, and even the birds around me are golden. The birds and butterflies look like solid gold flying around while the air has billions of glittery gold particles filling the atmosphere. One inch from my eyes there is gold floating, and fifty feet from my eyes there is gold floating. This is God's amazing generosity at work. This is a little bit of heaven being shown here on earth, however, without knowing and maintaining the same frequency as God's spirit, we are not able to see such splendor. Maintaining the same frequency means having more of His Spirit in me than not. In my opinion, it is mainly about meeting Him in His presence and Glory on a regular basis. Each individual can have a unique experience dwelling with Jesus on His Spirit level. The question is, who will take the time and effort to meet Him in such a place? Without His presence, we cannot achieve the truth that is exposed to us through our spirits which translates to our brains. To understand these theories we must be only one with Him, come in alignment with that of God's word, and be ready to handle the exposure of the truth. When Jesus speaks of giving us more of a measure of His faith, He discerns what we are ready for. With more faith comes more understanding of truth, and with that comes a tighter grasp of supernatural reality that many are not ready for. Those that see the world, live in the world, and live by feelings or emotions cannot fathom the concept with the depths of substance that make up His spirit. Also those that are scholars and philosophers like Plato or Confucius, understand the theory, but have a lack of faith to experience the supernatural side of God's wonder.

For some, even grasping our own authority over the demonic realm and demonic beings is too big of a force to hold on to. It is ok. God knows the exact timing to bestow these understandings upon individuals. I am grateful that He has shown me slowly step by step, with gentle nudges of love, to get me where I am today. I also look forward to the new things He is preparing to show me. We never stop learning or growing in Christ. It is an amazing journey to be on, with access to the Holiest of Holy Father God. How then do we access this supernatural wisdom that He chooses to give, bits at a time as he sees fit? Well since you have asked, the more time we spend living in the Spirit, unified with God the creator, Jesus as Spirit, God as Spirit (because God as man has already ascended) the more we become like Him. Are we all gods? No, but it is He that lives in us.

It is in each of us to hold the power and wisdom of God because of His love for us. It is in us to continue to thrive on the same frequency as God because of our love for Him.

We can move in all the ways Jesus did when He was flesh. Jesus would often go away alone to pray and to be unified with God. For hours He would unite with God in heaven, therefore, His flesh became minute compared to His Spirit. This type of example reminds me of when Moses went to the top of Mount Sinai, leaving his people behind, to enter the Glory of God. He did this to bring us the very laws of God himself,!. Moses came down off that mountainside with a glowing face. He had been so closely exposed to the glory of God that He himself had begun to take on God's spirit overriding his own flesh. God does amazing things when we spend time with Him alone.

We can also look at some examples of being in the spirit to the point of being transported to another geographic location, in this realm, or in another. I have heard stories of Godly people praying and being scooped up by Jesus and taken to distant lands to minister to those in need. This type of situation is incredible if you really think about it. People's complete body mass being lifted and taken to a place thousands of miles away is only something God could do. It surpasses all theories of time and space travel. I suppose one would have to be in a realm of God's glory for Him to do such an amazing thing. This is in the same bracket as being at a revival meeting with thousands of people, when the crowd falls over from a blast of the Holy Spirit. Our actual flesh and weight matters not. Peter walked the streets where they had brought forth the sick, and laid them on beds and couches. With the touch of Peter's shadow, people were healed. This is something to aspire toward as a disciple, but more importantly something we all need to get a grasp of if we are going to be able to withstand the end times as they approach. God's glory being of utmost importance, knowing God's voice better than our own, deciphering between satan's voice and our own, and manifesting on earth the Kingdom of God for all to partake; these are just a few tools we will need in our belt to fulfill the duty of being His bride.

God is a God of the supernatural. I like to think of this as a hyper-extended form of natural. If He so chooses, He can bypass and surpass any and all natural laws that He created originally. The laws in which our earth was based upon, like laws of gravitation and relativity, quantum mechanics, or geophysical laws (just to name a few) can be easily bypassed by God to ensure whatever He is planning. I personally think that He does this sort of thing when He performs a miracle. He has no time restraints or limits of any kind, hence, there is nothing weighing in on the final decision of God. My point here is that the more we get to know Him, the more we gain understanding that he is "I AM." There is a trust in this that will go deeper than any perception our human minds can fathom. Everything was made for Him, from Him and by Him, leaving much less of an accent on anything we think we are doing or can do. It is not about us. It is all about Him. I realize it is hard for us to wrap our minds around this idea, but if God graciously allows that to happen, we will in turn not limit God and be pleased with the outcome. It is beyond freeing when you can be in a place of simply trusting God. Trusting Him with no time limit, no desire of our own, and no certain way that it must go. To put absolutely no limits on God would allow us to gain a new perspective that would lead to an elevated walk with

Christ. It all starts with dying to self. It all starts with having no wants of your own. It all starts with the "I AM."

Let's take a look at a woman in our lifetime that walked with the Spirit of God. Kathryn Kuhlman would wave her hand and the people would fall, or become drunk in the spirit of God.[7] Some would enter into a meditative worship, enter into visions, have visitations from heavenly beings or Jesus himself, and some even got to visit heaven. Why did this happen when this woman of God would speak? Why was she such a powerful influence for that time and why do her teachings continue to minister to many people today? Katherine was living in the Spirit rather than the flesh. God allowed her to be filled with His spirit to the point of it bursting out of her body into the earthly realm. If we are not disciplined in reading the Bible and getting revelation through His word, or not taking time to be still with Him, our flesh cannot physically contain an abundance of wisdom or glory, and so the gifts will be abused. They will be used out of order and in a twisted sinful way instead of a holy way. Let us pray and focus more on being one with the Spirit of God that hovered and created all things. This will slowly teach our brains and our spirits in preparation of the excessive exposure to His holy mysteries that will be revealed. We must be mature in our walk.

There are some Christians that are still eating "baby food" although they met Jesus years ago. Reading a devotional a day, or going to church on Sunday's isn't gonna cut it. I am not judging your walk or your journey, as my own was not so fast, but I am going to challenge you for the glory of God. If our walk isn't strong, if we're still choosing our lives instead of Jesus' life, we might as well hand our lives over to the radical groups and the antichrist now. This isn't to scare you, but it is a definite attempt to get you to understand that the time is nearing whether you are ready or not. Do you want to survive? Do you want to bring God the glory He deserves? Do you want to be seated in heavenly places with Him, and talk about the strategies that satan has to attack you, your children or family? If you answered yes to any of these, it is time to let the very presence of God take over your being and become a son of the most high. Become a royal heir of Him that created the world and everything in it. Without these actions, along with repentance, deliverance, and worship, you will fear for your life as the prophecies of the Bible continue to be fulfilled. This goes far beyond arguing over the things that have developed in this century. These things are important, however, in the times that are coming to pass, you will have to make many incredible choices. Imagine if you will, a volcano lying under the ground with just moments until it erupts and reaps destruction on the land. This prophecy that is strewn throughout the word of God is a volcano waiting to erupt. And when it does, we as the church, are to be protected and covered by Jesus, and we the church are to be prepared as the women with the lamps were. I urge you to prepare now for these choices, because whether you are ready or not, they are coming. Wouldn't it be of your best interest to be prepared since these events are inevitable?

I want to share with you something that God has taught me about who we are and who He is in us. I began a rather quick study of entropy. The whole basis that I began this study, stemmed off of something the Lord said to me one night. I had had a rough day, as the woes of life just cracked me under pressure. When I have days like this I simply run into my father's arms and cry. I had a small bite to eat for dinner as my appetite was small due to the stress of the day. I jumped in the shower, brushed my teeth and brushed my hair. I finally laid down my heavy head onto my bed. I began to think of things that I should pray for. " I should pray for this situation to go more smoothly, and for God to allow me to win the lottery!" I said to God. I continued for a good thirty minutes on praying for things that I thought would help improve my life. I thought that if God would fix these things, that I could then honor Him better with less to worry about. But at some point, He stopped me in my selfish banter and told me to pray for wisdom. I thought about it for a moment, laughing to myself because who doesn't need Gods wisdom? But just when I think I have Him figured out, He gives me a whole new perspective.

I fell asleep. I am guessing here, but I think I slept for maybe 2 hours, when He awakened me out of a sound sleep to say this, "There are key program codes created in us at the molecular structure before we are born, having that which we are to fulfill and live out, written on our DNA." I was half asleep trying to understand what the heck I was hearing in my ears! But He helped me open my eyes and write down word for word what He had said. I thought about this day and night for almost a week. I thought, "Why does God keep talking to me about DNA and scientific information? Why does He think I'm smart enough to understand any of this? This is not the first time he talked to me about DNA!" God knew that it would irritate me so much that I wouldn't stop praying and asking until I had an answer. So being the woman I am, I prayed and prayed but still no epiphany came. I was at the library working on this book, not thinking about DNA at all. I was actually focused on the chapter about deliverance, when out of nowhere, I hear, "Entropy." I looked at my daughter and asked her if she had ever heard of the word. She said that she hadn't, so I looked it up online. I actually don't know if I had ever heard this word before, but it was clear after researching, that the Lord knew exactly what He was saying. Online, I found the following definition for entropy[8]:

> The idea of entropy comes from a principle of thermodynamics dealing with energy. It usually refers to the idea that everything in the universe eventually moves from order to disorder, and *entropy* is the measurement of that change. The word *entropy* finds its roots in the Greek *entropia,* which means "a turning toward" or "transformation." The word was used to describe the measurement of disorder by the German physicist Rudolph Clausius and appeared in English in 1868. A common example of entropy is that of ice melting in water. The resulting change from formed to free, from ordered to disordered increases the entropy.

An article entitled: *Entropy in the Old Creation: Is the Universe Running Down?*[9] succinctly explains this in layman's terms:

> The Laws of Thermodynamics are discoveries, or observations, about our physical world. They originated with the study of steam (heat) engines in the last century and were formulated originally in mathematical form. The First Law of Thermodynamics states that energy and matter cannot be created or destroyed, but only converted from one form to another. The Second Law

describes the flow of energy in the universe, which is always observed to be "downhill"---from states of high availability to states of low availability. Both observation and theory show that the universe is indeed running down, like a clock spring gradually uncoiling as energy is dissipated by the escapement mechanism. Ordinarily this means that heat flows from high temperature "reservoirs" to low temperature "sinks." To reverse the process, (so that heat flows uphill from a cold reservoir to a hotter reservoir), one must put in additional external energy to "pump" heat from the low temperature reservoir into the warmer one. This is how refrigerators and air-conditioners work. They are heat pumps which require extra energy to do their job. In a local region heat pumps remove heat from a colder reservoir and transport it to a hotter reservoir. This is done at less than 100% efficiency and the overall "entropy" of the universe is increased. Other engines utilize heated fluid from a high temperature source which does useful work, delivering the exhaust fluid to a lower temperature sink. Again the efficiency is always less than 100% and the overall "entropy" of the universe increases.

An equivalent way of stating the Second Law of Thermodynamics has to do with order and complexity in the universe. Orderly systems of molecules represent low entropy systems, and with the passage of time the normal tendency of things is for such systems to become disorderly, chaotic, and randomized. (Crystals are not low entropy systems in general because the lattice structure of crystals can be easily specified by a simple instruction code. In contrast genetic codes found in living cells are very low entropy structures because they possess a very large amount of information). To bring order out of chaos, we must put in outside energy and also programming information. The instructions, blueprints, programming instructions contained in the genetic codes of living cells are a perfect example. The process of utilizing energy is always less than 100% efficient. Energy is wasted every time we build and operate an engine or a machine to do useful work. "Entropy always increases" is an axiom of physics which has been found to always be true.

In this excellent article, *Evolution Vs Creationism*[10], a Biblical perspective is illustrated:

> It has been established that in all physical processes, every ordered system tends over time to become more disorganized, and also to lose energy in the form of heat, and to slow down; ---everything gets old and wears out, or runs down. This increasing randomness, disorder, and cooling is called "Entropy," and this situation is described in physics by the "Second Law of Thermodynamics." We see this principle expressed in the Bible (in about one thousand BC), when it says (concerning God): ***"In the beginning you laid the foundations of the earth, and the heavens are the work of your hands. They will perish, but you remain; they will all wear out like a garment. Like clothing you will change them and they will be discarded. But you remain the same, and your years will never end"*** Psalm 102:25-27 (NIV).

We know that if the stars in the heavens get very old, they will all burn out and they will all undergo "heat-death" until everything in the universe cools off to the same temperature. In the first century AD, the apostle Paul brings out the same idea when he wrote, ***For the creation was subjected to frustration ...in hope that the creation itself will be liberated from its bondage to decay...*** Romans 8:20-21 (NIV).

The Bible precisely describes the modern Law of increasing Entropy, as the whole material universe relentlessly runs down and loses available usable energy, in a process of "decay."

Why do you think this is important information to understand? Why do you think God Himself is reaching out to me to let me know about our bodies and also our earth? I think it is pretty self- evident that the Lord is bringing this to light because these are the two things that we need. The first is a basic understanding of how our DNA and molecular structure was preordained specifically key-coded for us individually before the beginning of time, so that we can do exactly what He preordained for us to do. As it clearly stated in Romans 8:28-30 (NIV):

> ***And we know that in all things God works for the good of those who love him, who have been called according to His purpose. For those God foreknew, he also predestined to be conformed to the image of his Son, so that he would be the firstborn among many brothers. And those he predestined He also called; those he called he***

also justified; those He justified He also glorified.

Those of us that have been predestined to a life of living in the Spirit of Jesus; We have also been called. The writing on our DNA contains the precise assignments given to us by God himself at the beginning of our time. The calling is hearing and obeying that assignment when it is given to us. In the end, Jesus wins. He conquers all, regardless of what we do, say, or obey, however, I think it best if we fulfill our purposes here while on earth, to glorify Him. For those of you that struggle with purpose, either having one and not knowing if it is the right one, or not having one at all, now is the time to figure it out. I look back on studies and preaching from long ago, and they too spoke of the end times. They too spoke of Jesus' return as if it was right around the corner. Even in the Bible they spoke of it. So does this mean we are to sit by and idly watch the world and humanity crumble into an immoral pit of abomination? Of course not!

We know that He is coming. We know the things that we will endure because it is written, and if we believe we are God's heirs in His kingdom, then we must also believe He is coming and coming suddenly. Now if you don't believe in the Bible in its entirety, or as the word of God, then I am praying for you to get it now. We are running out of time, and it is deep within you if you dare to look. God has waited this long because He loves us so much. He is gracefully giving us time to do as He has asked of us. It is encoded in our DNA remember! Ask Him to share with you exactly what yours says, and you can begin fulfilling your assignments to please and glorify your creator and Father.

5 NEW WORLD ORDER, LET'S TALK POLITICS

How will you nurture your children? How will you give them sustenance to grow and warmth to thrive if you cannot go to a grocery store or buy anything to fulfill these needs? How will you take your child or yourself to a doctor if you aren't able to do so unless you get the "Mark of the Beast?" For those of you that aren't familiar with the "Mark" it will benefit you greatly to read about it now. Revelation 13:16-17 (KJV) is a start:

> ***And he causeth all, both small and great, rich and poor, free and bond, to receive a mark in their right hand, or in their foreheads: And that no man might buy or sell, save he that had the mark, or the name of the beast, or the number of his name.***

Now I could go on for hours about the strategy, concepts and propaganda associated with the Mark of the Beast, but I will spare you all. However, I do think it is rather important to touch upon the biblical point of view and how it is correlating with today's scientific world, as well as satan's agenda. There are many reasons this Mark is so important for us to understand, but knowing that it is ultimately for satan to have control of all mankind, as well as to show us that we are in fact living in the end times according to the Holy Bible is definitely a playing factor. This Mark will control in a political, societal, religious, and spiritual way with the ultimate goal of a life separated from the presence of God. It is not to be mocked or underestimated but rather to be taken very seriously. I love how Revelation 13:18 explains that this man and plan must be contemplated. This riddle must be thought about and meditated upon. God was warning us that this mark and this beast can be exposed but we must rely on His Spirit of Wisdom in order to obtain such information. If the antichrist is the one that will deceive many with lying signs and wonders and also introduce the mark of the beast, then suffice it to say we had better use wisdom for these times ahead.

> ***This calls for wisdom: Let the one who has insight calculate the beast's number, for it is man's number, and his number is 666.*** Revelation 13:18 (NET)

The younger generations must be warned and taught properly as to not fall to technological advances of this century. Although there have been many ground-breaking advances in our twenty first century to help further along the human race, which replaces a reliance on the power of God. Because of such advances, the human race has developed a desire to become God. But this is not a coincidence by any means. The beast and his mark mentioned in the Bible are simply coming to pass through the means of a society using and relying on advanced technology. It is not surprising that satan would use science to fulfill his big moment on earth.

In an attempt to keep this portion of the book relatively simple, I will say only a few things to look out for, and hopefully that you all will pray and do your homework relating to the Mark of the Beast in affiliation with our day and age. In my opinion, radio frequency identification also referred to as the RFID chip, or identification tattoos could very well be the tool that may usher this beast into our existence. In 2007 there was a plan expressed by the government that by 2017 the human race would have an identification chip implanted in the right hand or the forehead. Although there are many reasons the chip was created, like healthcare systems, location services, medical history and even allowing full access to a person's bank account, there is also an evil agenda behind it. They are selling it to the public as a tool of convenience to buying things and making errands more time efficient as well as making lines at airports or hospitals nonexistent for the chip user. But understand my friends, that getting such a thing placed in your body has a much greater plan for the existence of human beings. Getting the chip will put you, your privacy, and your freedom in a questionable position, while spiritually placing your future in the hands of the devil.

CERN, the European Organization for Nuclear Research, whom we will discuss in a bit, created the World Wide Web, or www. After getting the RFID chip, the World Wide Web can interact with your bodies, collecting data and uploading your information into this sci-fi matrix. It not only could do so by using your "data," but it is also capable of tracking your health information, such as your hormone levels, disease progression, and even blood glucose levels. This will be a convenient tool to use when they decide to share with mankind that their technologies and scientific advances have found a way for us to live much longer, more fulfilling lives by changing our DNA. If you pay attention to the scientific, religious and political progression of things in the upcoming months, you will continue to see a parallel to the prophecies written in Revelation. If you remain in Him my friends, you will see how God is teaching us to heal the sick. It will be of great importance in the future. You will see how hearing His voice to reach a safe place to dwell could mean life or death. You will know that when you are hungry, that God will provide, but that your body is familiar with fasting as a way of life.

If you're only interested in love, and world peace, or unity and every religion respecting everyone else's religion, you are headed to very dangerous grounds. Before I get into the prophecies to come, let me first speak on what we will be facing if we, as God's church, cannot be almost completely filled with and utilizing the Holy Spirit.

What are the functions of the Holy Spirit? If you have been walking with the Lord for a while you may know the answer to this question, but it is imperative we understand His function to utilize it completely in our lives. It must become a place where the Holy Spirit has literally become part of our human body and spirit that you walk in the Lords footsteps. With almost no separation, the Holy Spirit makes a home inside of you. As a holy temple, your body is transformed from a sinful disgrace, to a perfect and righteous temple that holds the spirit of God! First of all the Holy Spirit exalts Yeshua Hamashiach, Jesus Christ! To exalt Him is to constantly raise Him to a higher level. To praise Him highly. To present to us in a way that is overly favorable. He is the highest ranked official of our lives, of the world, and of heaven, therefore, He is to always be, forever be, exalted. The Holy Spirit does this and then permeates into our lives. John 16:14 (NIV) says ***He will glorify me because it is from me that he will receive what he***

will make known to you.

The Holy Spirit communicates the message from the heart of the Lord. That which is deep in our very beings, comes to us through the Spirit of God. We are a blessed people to have a God that wants to communicate with us in such a significant way that He sent the spirit of His Son to always be present. Above all, His Glory is to be lifted as high as it can be through us. Now this is going to happen regardless of the stance we take on the matter, however, it was God's intension to have a personal, intimate relationship with us and to communicate all day every day. I realize this may seem like a huge mountain staring you in the face. To walk only in the Holy Spirit of God, all day long may seem not only impossible but unfathomable. It is something I personally am still striving to achieve. Yet each day, I allot more time, more worship, and more love. It is harder to distinguish me with the Holy Spirit versus me without. He is always talking, always sharing, and always helping us. Without the baptism of His Holy Spirit we cannot begin to understand this, so if any of you reading this have not yet been baptized in His Spirit, I urge you to do so.

This can be a very simple process where you just ask Jesus to baptize you and you ask for the Holy Spirit to come and live in you. You ask for His Spirit to penetrate your soul, spirit, mind and body. You can ask for an impartation of His Holy Spirit and give only Him permission to enter. If you attend a local non-denominational, spirit-filled church, someone there would be able to pray over you. You may be asking how a new world order has anything to do with baptism of His Holy Spirit, however, I feel it is an important plan of action to take so that we move in the anointing God has for us. He will be most glorified when He fulfills His purpose in us. This will be the beginning of a true journey with Christ. And to piggyback off of this action of being baptized in the Holy Spirit, He lives in us. ***Do you not know that you are a temple of God and that the Spirit of God dwells in you?*** 1 Corinthians 3:16 (NASB).

> ***And what union can there be between God's temple and idols? For we are the temple of the living God. As God said: "I will live with them and walk among them, and I will be their God, and they will be my people."***
> 2 Corinthians 6: 16 (NIV).

We have to allow His Spirit to dwell in us completely, not half- heartedly. Now I admit that this is easier said than done. There are many things opposing His spirit, around us, and possibly in us; Namely our flesh, our sin, our lack of obedience, lack of repentance and forgiveness, as well as satan and his unruly demons. By the end of this book I will touch upon each of these, however, it is important that you remember that they will give resistance to us living in the complete wholeness of Christ himself. This goal should be very high on our priority list.

"I will put My Spirit within you and cause you to walk in My statutes, and you will be careful to observe My ordinances."
Ezekiel 36:27 (NASB).

I would say that scripture makes it very clear that the Holy Spirit of God dwells within us. Why is this so important? There are many reasons for the Holy Spirit's importance of dwelling in us, but one I would like to point out now is for that of discernment. This is a spiritual gift given from God. In my opinion, this is one of the most important gifts necessary for the end times. Let's discuss the scripture that explains this as a gift from the Lord. In 1 Corinthians 12:7-14 (KJV) it states the following:

> ***But the manifestation of the Spirit is given to every man to profit withal. For to one is given by the Spirit the word of wisdom; to another the word of knowledge by the same Spirit; To another faith by the same Spirit; to another the gifts of healing by the same Spirit; To another the working of miracles; to another prophecy; to another discerning of spirits; to another diverse kinds of tongues; to another the interpretation of tongues: But all these worketh that one and the selfsame Spirit, dividing to every man severally as he will. For as the body is one, and hath many members, and all the members of that one body, being many, are one body: so also is Christ. For by one Spirit are we all baptized into one body, whether we be Jews or Gentiles, whether we be bond or free; and have been all made to drink into one Spirit. For the body is not one member, but many.***

This scripture is loaded with information of the gifts that we are given, why they are given to us, the possibilities of how many are given, and the reasons they are given! What an amazing word from God we have here. Sticking to the subject of the discernment of spirits, and the importance of it, let's discuss how it signifies a correlation with end times and preparation. This gift allows us to speak to the Father, and hear what spirits are tormenting a person. This gift allows us to speak to the Father and hear what demon, or principality is causing these negative effects in humans and nations. Are you aware that soon, if not already, super humans are coming? People will be taking direct instructions from satan because his "DNA" will be in them? Are you aware of the super human armies, or super soldiers that will soon be released on earth to enforce the command of a one world order? Let us now delve into some crazy conspiracy theory; science non-fiction. This is a focused look at what is to come.

What the government, CERN, DARPA, Papal influences, and the current global vision for the future of mankind has become in our time here on earth is intense. The necessity of our spiritual lives and preparation are directly related to the end times that are coming upon us faster than ever.

I want to talk now about DARPA. This is the "Defense Advanced Research Projects Agency." This agency is in part, the people that are developing super humans by genetically modifying them. What does this mean? They are genetically modifying human genes to create very specific abilities to be placed in humans. This is being done for many reasons. It is an army that is being formed for the end.

> ***And the number of the army of the horsemen were two hundred thousand thousand: and I heard the number of them.***
> Revelation 9:16 (KJV).

Now I mostly agree with the following opinion that from a blog article *All Hell Breaks Loose (Revelation 9:1-21).*[11]

> It is worth noting that the massive army of 200 million is often thought to be a reference to China. While this may be possible, it is more likely that this army is not human but demonic. These are hellish horsemen riding satanic steeds. Several reasons support this: (1) The fifth and sixth trumpet judgments go together since they are called the first two of three "woes." Since the fifth trumpet is clearly demonic, it is fairly certain the sixth trumpet is as well. (2) Fallen angels, like those of the fifth trumpet judgment, lead this army (9:15). Since the leaders are four fallen angels, it makes sense that the troops they are leading are also demons. (3) There are other examples in Scripture of supernatural armies (e.g., 2 Kings 2:11; 6:13-17; Revelation 19:11, 14). (4) The weapons mentioned—fire, sulfur, and smoke—are always supernatural weapons in the Bible and are associated with hell, four times in Revelation (14:10-11; 19:20; 20:10; 21:8).

While I mostly agree with this blog article, I feel there is a chance that these soldiers may not be 100% demonic. An army that will have faster runners than ever in existence. An army that will have the ability to re-grow limbs. These soldiers will have no mercy because of the extraction of any empathy genes, and controlling of the mind in every way. Their abilities will be so enhanced they will move like gods. They will move with the power of satan himself, but could they be part human? There has been large amounts of monies given to Universities in the US to allow studying and development of these various types of defilation of the human, God-made, genes. Genes have been removed from animals and inserted into humans in order to give them certain chromosomal aspects that the animal holds. There are not only negative scientific and biological effects that will plague humans, but obviously serious spiritual detriment. Long-term consequences of altering human genes will be put into place the same way God did in the days of Noah when He wiped out the earth. Yes some positive attributes may come from it like having no disease and being able to live longer or indefinitely, there is no point if the world ends and only your spirit matters.

Although we can speculate with opinions, I prefer here to stick to the biblical perspective only. Science is amazing, yes, however, the Bible shows to be true when it comes up against any science that strives to disprove it. Therefore, the importance on biblically sound prophecies is much more important to the believer than discussing or even arguing science. According to the Transhumanism website[12]:

> Transhumanism is a way of thinking about the future that is based on the premise that the human species in its current form does not represent the end of our development but rather a comparatively early phase.
>
> Transhumanism is a loosely defined movement that has developed gradually over the past two decades.
>
> "Transhumanism is a class of philosophies of life that seek the continuation and acceleration of the evolution of intelligent life beyond its currently human form and human limitations by means of science and technology, guided by life-promoting

principles and values:" -Max More (1990)

This my friend, is a precise depiction of what is currently happening in our world. It has actually been happening for quite some time now, but it is being exposed more and more. It is my understanding that this is what God was referring to when He spoke about the end being like that in the days of Noah. The scripture says in Luke 17:26-36 (NIV):

> ***"Just as it was in the days of Noah, so also will it be in the days of the Son of Man. People were eating, drinking, marrying and being given in marriage up to the day Noah entered the ark. Then the flood came and destroyed them all. It was the same in the days of Lot. People were eating and drinking, buying and selling, planting and building. But the day Lot left Sodom, fire and sulfur rained down from heaven and destroyed them all. It will be just like this on the day the Son of Man is revealed. On that day no one who is on the housetop, with possessions inside, should go down to get them. Likewise, no one in the field should go back for anything. Remember Lot's wife! Whoever tries to keep their life will lose it, and whoever loses their life will preserve it. I tell you, on that night two people will be in one bed; one will be taken and the other left. Two women will be grinding grain together; one will be taken and the other left."***

This leads us to many different feelings I assume, but one of the first thoughts I had was "what happened in the days of Noah?" What was the thing that was happening in this time? Is that what is happening today in our world? Let us now take a look at Genesis 6:1-4 (KJV):

> ***And it came to pass, when men began to multiply on the face of the earth, and daughters were born unto them, That the sons of God saw the daughters of men that they were fair; and they took them wives of all which they chose. And the Lord said, My spirit shall not always strive with man, for that he also is flesh: yet his days shall be an hundred and twenty years. There were giants in the earth in those days; and also after that, when the sons of God came in unto the daughters of men, and they bare children to them, the same became mighty men which were of old, men of renown.***

Although this scripture has raised much controversy for many years, the majority of Rabbi's believed that this had really happened. The sons of God were angels. According to *Let us Reason Ministries*[13]:

> The Hebrew word for sons of God is Bene Elohim. This term for angels occurs four times in the old Testament in the Septuagent version (the Greek translation of the Hebrew scriptures) it's meaning is always used as angels of God, never of man. Most scholars believe this event describes a union between fallen angels who cohabitated with human females. This unnatural occurrence of combining two different species resulted in an offspring of what are called 'giants' in the King James and NKJ version

and Nephilim in the NAS, and the English translation of the Jewish Masoretic text.

Now how does fallen angels having sex with women have anything to do with how the "Days of Noah" relate to the times of Jesus' return? It is quite clear that through this scripture, the angels that had sex with human women were also having babies. These babies, the Nephilim, were the giants in the land. I want to break down this word Nephilim. According to ***Strong's Concordance*** (H5303), Nephilim: immediately refers us to the word "giants," I am pointing this out because it speaks in the scripture in Genesis 6:8-13 (KJV):

> ***But Noah found grace in the eyes of the Lord. These are the generations of Noah: Noah was a just man and perfect in his generations, and Noah walked with God. And Noah begat three sons, Shem, Ham, and Japheth. The earth also was corrupt before God, and the earth was filled with violence. And God looked upon the earth, and behold, it was corrupt; for all flesh had corrupted his way upon the earth. And God said unto Noah, The end of all flesh is come before me; for the earth is filled with violence through them; and behold, I will destroy them with the earth.***

Here is God's text saying that ***Noah was a just man and perfect in his generations.*** In Hebrew, this word generations literally means generations. Translated perfectly it means "without blemish." There were no defects in his gene pool if you will. What defects have we seen in the gene pool here in Genesis? The Fallen Angels making babies with man. That was the defect then, which is why God wiped out the world with a flood.

Let's jump to current time and assume that with the movement of DARPA and transhumanism, the perfect genetics that man holds are being altered with DNA from that of other species. Whether it be that of animals, that of scientific alterations, or that of fallen angels will tell in due time. I am under the opinion that all three are being done, but that the worst to come is that of the fallen angels just like in the times of Noah.

Let us now discuss CERN. According to Wikipedia,[14] this is:

> The European Organization for Nuclear Research, known as CERN, is a European research organization that operates the largest particle physics laboratory in the world. They created a machine called Large Hadron Collider or LHC that will fuse together sub-atomic particles almost reaching the speed of light. This machine is on the French-Swiss border and is buried deep below the surface. It is approximately 575 feet below the earth. The tunnel in which it sits is about 17 miles long.

They search for the "God particle." For a very broad definition of the "God particle", this is that which occurred in the formation of the earth. Having a biblical perspective, God spoke it into existence. This is truth. However, they, for years have been researching and testing this machine smashing together atoms, as well as other intricate scientific terms, to recreate conditions similar to those during the creation of the universe. This will in turn allow us access into other dimensions. Other supernatural spheres that have been hidden from us for a reason. Once this portal is open, things can come and go, and although their hope was to be able to open and close at their desired times, if they failed at this, it becomes an open portal from the demonic realm to our own. The place in France where this machine is somewhat located is called Saint- Genus-Poilly which comes from the Latin "Appolliacum."[15] It is said that in Roman times this was a direct temple for that of Apollo, and that the people that lived there believed it was a direct gateway to the underworld.

I want to now take an in depth journey with John the revelator as he spoke of a vision that was given to him in the book of Revelation. In Revelation 9: 1-12 (KJV):

> *And the fifth angel sounded, and I saw a star fall from heaven unto the earth: and to him was given a key of the bottomless pit. And he opened the bottomless pit; and there arose a smoke out of the pit as the smoke of a great furnace; and the sun and the air were darkened by reason of the smoke of the pit. And there came out of the smoke locusts upon the earth: and unto them was given power, as the scorpions of the earth have power. And it was commanded them that they should not hurt the grass of the earth neither any green thing, neither any tree; but only those men which have not the seal of God in their foreheads. And to them it was given that they should not kill them, but that they should be tormented five months: and their torment was as*

the torment of a scorpion, when he striketh a man. And in those days shall men seek death, and shall not find it; and shall desire to die, and death shall flee from them. And the shapes of the locusts were like unto horses prepared unto battle; and on their heads were as it were crowns like gold, and their faces were as the faces of men. And they had hair as the hair of women, and their teeth were as the teeth of lions. And they has breastplates, as it were breastplates of iron; and the sound of their wings was as the sound of chariots of many horses running to battle. And they had tails like unto scorpions, and there were stings in their tails: and their power was to hurt men five months. And they had a king over them, which is the angel of the bottomless pit, whose name in the Hebrew tongue is Abaddon, but in the Greek tongue has his name Apollyon.

God loves to speak to us when we do nothing at all too. What I mean by this is that He chooses when to speak and how to speak. I have been asking for many years now for Him to take me up to heaven for a little bit to hang out with Him, yet it hasn't happened yet, but I am confident He will do it someday. However, on the other side of this spectrum, there have been many times that He surprises me with a vision, or something else supernatural when I didn't ask for it. He has shown me different terrains in Heaven, but have yet to be with Him up there. I believe it is all about our calling and our dying to self that often initiates lessons from the Father.

A few years ago, I was awakened late one evening,

only to look up and see my whole room filled with something very unusual. They were 3D-like, glowing boxes, attached to strands. To me it looked like some small ladders and something I vaguely remembered from science class. They were glowing with illumination. Too many different colors to count. I just gazed at their beauty for as long as I could, and then my eyes shut, and I drifted back to sleep. When I woke up the next morning, it was still vivid in my mind! I was so grateful for such a beautiful vision. But I was a bit confused with what I was seeing. So I asked God, "God, I love what you showed me last night, but what was it?" I heard the word polyhedron. Now I am certainly no expert in geometry, or mathematics, but I knew this was a shape. However, that is all I knew. So I pulled out my trusty phone and googled the word polyhedron. As I was looking at pictures, I thought to myself that it looked similar but not exactly what I had seen. Then I heard the words "polyhedron, strand, changing DNA." So again I googled it. There it was! Exactly what I saw. I was so excited that I had found what God was showing me, although I didn't yet understand the point. I prayed and prayed to figure out what changing DNA meant. I pondered whether it was God changing my DNA to make me more like Him. I contemplated whether He meant other people's DNA was changing. It took over a month. I finally understood. I began researching the purpose of a mesh polyhedron sequence. This is what I read in an article regarding *Integrated DNA Technologies*[16]:

> At the Karolinska Institute, in Stockholm, Sweden, Dr. Bjorn Hogberg's laboratory (www.hogberglab.net) studies nanoscale engineering with DNA. Using self-assembly properties of DNA, the scientists wanted to create DNA scaffolds. As

one application, the team envisioned using these nanostructures for exact positioning of proteins and other molecules. Such technology could potentially be applied to create protein patterns to study cell signaling, deliver drugs, produce very pure DNA oligonucleotides enzymatically. And build DNA devices like molecular sensors.

To execute some of these applications, the team needed a tool to make very general shapes out of DNA. Using current DNA origami methods, it is already possible to generate many different shapes on the nanoscale level. However, Dr. Hogberg hoped to simplify existing methods. He explains, "What we really wanted to do was develop a method by which you could simply sit down at your computer, draw a 3D shaped imaging shape in 3D imaging software, and then convert it to DNA. The process is analogous to macroscopic 3D printing methods, where you use computer software to draw a 3D structure, and a 3D printer to produce your structure in plastic, metal, and even cells.

Now I assure you I know nothing about molecular structures, DNA strands or helixs', or extensive engineering mathematics, but what I do know something about is my Lord, Jesus. When I read and researched this matter, a lot of it was like reading Chinese to me. But certain things definitely stuck out, even to me, with my average sized brain. This is about the changing of DNA. This is about possibly producing new cells in DNA. I still wasn't sure where God was going with all of this until the day I came upon DARPA and the breakdown of genetic modifications that are being done. This was enough for me to take all of this very seriously.

It all made sense how in the days of Noah, the fallen angels, the one world order, and even the super soldiers play such a significant role in today's time.

Having said all of this, I hope that you are asking yourself that if challenged by soldiers that aren't even human how you will fight them. I guarantee you that weapons of this world will not work. Guns, fire, knives and even hiding will not work. They will be able to find you with their supernatural senses and their bodies will be too advanced to be wounded. There will be one way to survive them and it is Jesus. In the name of Jesus, using the authority given you by Jesus whom you sit next to in heavenly places, you will be able to defeat them. You must begin activating the gifts God has given you for such a time as this. Now do you see why discernment of spirits is of utmost importance? It will become an easy thing to call the demon's name out and bind it right there as it stands to kill you. Begin to put your gifts into practice if you are not already!

I spend a lot of my day binding demons so they cannot alter or influence my day in any way. Although binding is a temporary solution to a problem. Complete deliverance of the demons is so necessary for two reasons. The first reason is because demons are constantly working through people in this world to deter us from God's lighted path, and if I tie them up, they cannot interfere. Hence this leads me to a day of obedience and intimacy with the Lord! I do this whenever and wherever I feel the Lord directs me to do so. God has shown me that even though we have beautiful people in this world, and beautiful people who have good intentions, they also have demons. Their demons have nothing but bad motives and plans for them and would love to have an effect on you too if they are capable. It is a necessary tool at times to bind demons over people you love in order to walk in Christ's path. I will give a short example of this that may disturb some of you, however, I feel God wants me to share this lesson that has helped me for years.

I had just started going to a new church that was everything I had hoped for. The people were amazing! They were full of love, joy, and generosity. The word was being preached, and the Spirit of God was moving there. I thought all was well, and for the most part it was. But after getting closer to some of the people, God began to give me dreams. He began to wake me up night after night with concerning dreams involving people from my church. The first night it was a dream about a woman doing bonafide witchcraft spells on me from her home. God showed me that she had grown up doing magic but that she was a Christian in a charismatic church as well. The following evening God showed me another woman in the church saying prayers that were not in alignment with His will. She would often pray for me and the church leaders with prayers of good intention, but not listening to the Holy Spirit to guide her with appropriate prayers. As a result, she was praying witchcraft prayers for people without even being aware. As God showed me some of the people that were doing rebellious things knowingly and unknowingly, He began to pinpoint reasons this was happening. He showed me that there were generational curses involved for some and for others there were demons influencing them. God opened my spiritual eyes to see the specific demons that were influencing these people, the same way He showed me when I would minister on the streets. So as He showed me these things I was confused on how I was supposed to protect myself. I was also upset that I had to protect myself from the body of God. He assured me that His Spirit worked through them in a great way, but that demons also were working in them. He humbled me and said "Kristina, do you not sin against me?" I thought about it and of course I said "yes" with sadness in my heart. Then He said "Kristina, do I not use you for my kingdom?" I then understood that I was just like these people with my own sin and own demons.

After He humbled me to this notion, He started to put the lesson into action so that I could begin overcoming the problem instead of judging people. It was not the easiest thing for me to wrap my head around, but He made it easy to understand one Sunday morning. When I pulled into the parking lot of the church, I clearly heard God say to bind one person's demons before entering the church. I couldn't believe it, but then again it made so much sense. If during intercessory prayer we can bind demons over those we pray for and ask God to move powerfully in their lives, then why wouldn't He allow us to bind demons over saved people that were being influenced by darkness? This was a very new concept for me, but I knew it was the Lord that was speaking. I decided to obey God and bind all the demons that He named. I bound them from talking to me and looking at me. Of course, I did so with Jesus Christ's authority.

I got out of the car and walked into the church. As I went into the sanctuary to join in worship, this person walked by me. She said nothing and didn't even look at me. I thought for sure that she was in a rush to worship and must not have seen me. To my surprise, the service ended, we mingled showing love to our church family, but not once did this woman look at me. This was definitely unusual for her. She always spoke to me. She always had some word or Godly advice to give me. Even on off days, she would at least say hello to me and greet me with a hug. But today, she did nothing. I went home thinking about what had happened. How curious this made me. Had God trusted me with such a secret that even my brothers and sisters have demons trying to sidetrack me from my purpose? I of course had to take a look at myself and wonder if I too had demons that were speaking through me to other people.

This was a very important lesson that I learned and has been imperative in my walk. I have had to stay accountable to Jesus with my own sin and demons and do monthly maintenance on myself with deliverance. I have also helped some of my brothers and sisters to open their eyes to this lesson and they began to protect themselves. Sometimes we Christians get into a routine of being "holier than thou" which allows demons to put a bit of influence in our lives. It is sometimes very hard for saved people to humble themselves to the point of knowing that their sin causes demons to work through them. There are many people who will tell you that they have overcome with the help of Jesus That does not mean that satan can't impress things upon you. If you have sin in your life, which we all do, then he has a legal right to be there until repentance takes place. Remember that church family. As I struggled with this portion of the book, God said "Get thee behind me satan!" I immediately knew what He wanted me to reference here. Lets take a look at Matthew 16:21-23 (NET):

> ***From that time on Jesus began to show his disciples that he must go to Jerusalem and suffer many things at the hands of the elders, chief priests, and experts in the law, and be killed, and on the third day be raised. So Peter took him aside and began to rebuke him: "God***

> ***forbid, Lord! This must not happen to you!" But he turned and said to Peter, "Get behind me, satan! You are a stumbling block to me, because you are not setting your mind on God's interests, but on man's."***

There are two things here that stand out to me for the purposes of this portion of the book. The first is that God is showing us that as a Christ follower, we are more than capable of saying a prayer that goes against the very will of God. Jesus will correct us when we do this. It is simply rebellion to do so. Secondly, Jesus spoke to satan here, not Peter, showing that followers of Jesus can have satan influencing them. If we are to move as Jesus did, then we too must take authority over demons and satan. We must do this always and on whomever. Jesus didn't limit His rebuke because Peter was His follower, rather, He rebuked the evil that was influencing Him to further the Kingdom of God, and so too, shall we. And although sin must be resisted with abhorrence, it is out of love that the evil must be eliminated and I feel strongly that we must not take it personally. We must get very low and stay very low to humbly acknowledge the strategies that God uses.

It is my friendship with Jesus that teaches me these things. It is not the gifts or the demons or even the church that is the secret, but it is my friendship with Christ that brings understanding. So as you contemplate these chapters and topics, know that the most important thing of all is your close friendship with your Creator.

6 KINGDOM OF DARKNESS

I feel it important to discuss satan and his demons, not to glorify him or to give him attention in any way, rather to understand how he and his soldiers work in our lives. It is imperative to know the strategy of satan as well as which demons are doing what to us, and how. I realize this is a topic most Christians and non-Christians like to avoid. Sometimes I feel that people are completely dismissive of satan. I have had so many conversations with Bible believing Christians that live their lives knowing nothing about satan. I would say bravo, but since God has made it my particular calling to remove demons that come from satan, I cannot just ignore the fact that he is there. I can perhaps understand how non-Christians may hold beliefs that dismiss satan, but Christians? Bible-believing, born-again, spirit-filled Christians? How is this even possible? The purpose of this book is not to try to convince anyone of anything, but rather to speak the truth and the truths of the Bible and let God fill in the blanks. It does make sense how our world has gotten so far away from God when I think about how much damage satan does on a daily basis. When the majority of God's own church are sitting back and allowing it to happen. We are lacking a courageousness in Christ due to fear, and most assuredly, a complete and utter blinding oppression from that which we call the devil! I pray that this book will bring some divine wisdom to the table!

Understand that satan and his demons know you, they study you, and they are roaming around waiting to devour you. They go to God in heaven accusing you of what sins you have committed daily against God. It is best to know your nemesis. Know the ground from which he fights, understand the availability and entrance points he has to contaminate you and your family. In my life, this has been one of the most powerful tools God has shown me thus far in my walk with Him. I would like to share part of my testimony before we all take authority and use it against satan, his servants, and his agenda.

When I was 17 years old, Christ changed my life in a major way. I was raised Catholic and brought up in the Catholic religion with Catholic traditions. I was baptized as a baby, which in the Catholic religion is the belief that my soul is saved from that point on. I then endured Catechism as a child. I say endured because I could never relate to what I was being taught. Merriam-Webster defines Catechism as:

> A collection of questions and answers that are used to teach people about the Christian religion: A book that explains the beliefs of the Christian religion by using a list of questions and answers.

That sounds nice, however my experience in this wasn't exactly like that of this definition. We were taught some things about the Christian religion, yes, however, we were also taught about the Catholic beliefs which differ from biblical views. I don't remember much about these classes except that I was a bit rebellious about the teachings. I was told that I would never go to heaven if I continued to act the way I acted, or kept the attitude that I had. That is the unfortunate memory I have of this period of my life. I spend many years praying to the saints. We would pray to Saint Anthony when we lost something, or pray to the Virgin Mary for guidance, or to Saint Michael for protection. I remember when I was sixteen and I got my very first boyfriend. Oh the delight of trying to understand love as a teenager! I wouldn't wish it upon anyone! I hit a point where I was desperate and at the end of my rope. I wanted God to intervene to give me what I thought was the best thing for my life. For the sake of privacy, we'll call him Gregory. He was a playboy that never understood my devotion or love for him. He was an unfaithful boy that was manipulative and had many of his own issues to deal with. He almost wrecked me.

I remember needing God's help so much that I did what any Catholic would do. I prayed to the Virgin Mary statue that sat on my mother's dresser. It was about 2 inches tall, plastic, and the color of her blue dress was faded and rubbed off, perhaps from my mother praying as she held the statue. I cried out "Oh Virgin Mary! Please, please, please, fix my relationship! Make us better! Let us be together forever." As time passed, nothing changed. As a matter of fact, things got a bit worse. I was furious. I was hurt and angry that the Virgin Mary or God or Jesus didn't help me and my situation. I didn't understand why my mother would pray and pray when it didn't work! I continued to rely on my own knowledge and craftiness along with manipulation to get things I wanted from Gregory. But this too did not work completely. There were glimpses of success, but they all turned out to be temporary.

I walked along blind in the world attempting to use

my own will to get what I wanted for about a year, until the day I was drawn to the supernatural world. I loved horror movies, and I loved to be the leader. What I mean by this is that whenever we would have sleepovers, or hang out with my friends or siblings, I would initiate playing with the Ouija board. I would initiate doing séances and contacting the dead. I remember doing some levitation thing that actually worked and I was floating above the ground. It was so much fun to me. I remember times when playing with the Ouija board that we would speak to a particular spirit. His name I will keep to myself, but we would ask him questions, and best believed he answered them. We would ask how he died, where he lived, and what he wanted to tell us. One day things got very interesting when we asked him to tell us how many trophies were in the room next to us. He answered correctly and I was intrigued! It was exciting to ask questions and get immediate answers. Back and forth I went to Catholic Church to Ouija boards. Then as I grew in age, I had to begin thinking about my future. What college would I attend, and what would my major be. How would I move to another state for college without my beloved Gregory? This all took precedence over what once was a fun game of talking to the dead. So in the interim of high school and college, I was perplexed and stressed with life, and Gregory!

My brother, who is four years older than I, came home from college for a holiday visit. He began telling my siblings and me that he had met a man. He met a man named Jesus, and that Jesus has changed his life in a significant way. He was so excited about Jesus. He told me that if I just gave my life to Christ, it would change. I rebutted saying that I knew Jesus. I said "We were brought up Catholic, of course I know Jesus." He assured me that it was different. He began telling me of these supernatural things that were happening in his life. Of course, I was intrigued to say the least; it was supernatural! So when he explained that he had spoken in a language he hadn't known previously, and then he told awesome stories about seeing demons, I was very interested in knowing what this was all about.

Soon after, I watched my sister give her life to Christ and saw changes occur in her as well. So one day, I was hurting and about to give up on my relationship and everything that disappointed me and I took the challenge. I said "Jesus, if your real, show me!" It was a slow process, but each day I began to hear and understand more of what my siblings were saying about Jesus. Things seemed clearer to me somehow. I decided to attend a non-denominational church after giving my heart to Jesus. In this particular service the pastor was imparting the gift of the Holy Spirit upon people. I nervously walked to the front of the church, quivering a bit and said "Please pray that prayer for me." He began to impart the Holy Spirit upon me and I immediately started to speak in an unknown language. I thought of my brother's experience and I was excited to see that God can give us all these different supernatural gifts. I began to study the Bible and talk to God on a regular basis. Things seemed better than ever! It was just about time for me to go off to college and I told Gregory we were done if he didn't attend college in the city where I was moving.

It was all working out for me! Until, one day things got strange. I was fervently praying for spiritual gifts. I was so drawn to the supernatural world I had known before, that I desired the supernatural world that God had to offer. In this adventure, I remember walking down the street in Pittsburgh, PA one random afternoon.

It was a normal day, and I was running simple errands. I looked across the street and saw a man walking to the bus stop, when the most peculiar thing happened. A strange shape, dark and detailed, emerged above his head. I thought to myself, "Am I crazy?" I was looking around to see the amazement on other people's faces. But no one else seemed to notice. They continued to walk as if nothing was going on! I couldn't believe it. How can no one see this awful looking creature above this man's head? So I carefully studied this creature from across the street. I didn't feel I was in danger; I was truly curious. I went home and decided to look up scripture that may explain what was going on. I began to understand that what I had seen was a demon. One of satan's minions. I wasn't sure why I saw it, but nevertheless it was quite an experience. The days passed and I was constantly looking to see if there were any of these things on any one I knew, or on random people on the streets. But to my dismay, it didn't happen again. I proceeded to pray for enlightenment on this, and also for my gifts to manifest.

My sister and her friend decided to come to Pittsburgh for a Christian conference that I was unable to attend. However, one night we were praying on the floor in my apartment that yet another amazing thing happened. Our eyes were closed as we lifted up God Jehovah with praise. For one reason or another I opened my eyes to one of the most beautiful things I had ever seen. There was a huge, shining angel standing among us! It was glorious and larger than life! It was my first experience with seeing a holy being. Even though this was almost 20 years ago, I still thank God for that experience today. How honored I felt! How blessed was I! These new experiences were simply fascinating to me and continued to keep me amazed at what God could show me.

One evening I was alone in my dorm room, most likely just finishing some homework or having a quick snack before bed. I was resting with my eyes closed (attempting to fall asleep,) when I heard something strange. It was a shuffling on the carpet. It sent chills through my body. I slowly pulled the blanket just below my eyes. When I summoned enough strength, I slowly pulled the covers down and looked to my right expecting to see a huge monster next to my bed. Nothing was there. The sound continued, and as it got louder, I assumed it was getting closer. I was frozen with fear, knowing that some unknown, supernatural creature was right next to me. At this moment I asked God to take away the gift. It was all I could think of. I felt I had just gone a bit out of my element. I thought that maybe I asked for more than I could chew. I called my brother and told him all about what had happened. He asked me what sins I had committed to allow this demonic being to affect me. I thought of a few, as I hadn't yet dealt with certain things in my life. This was a definitive new view of sin for me, and I took it much more seriously from this point on. After this my life became relatively normal again. I could no longer see into the supernatural realm, and although I had very strong intuitions regularly, my supernatural life as I had known it was gone. It seemed like a distant memory.

I walked the earth not knowing what was around me, and quite frankly; not caring. I decided it was time to leave my beloved Gregory and live a life of abstinence for Jesus. In doing this, somewhere along the way, I began regularly seeing his best friend. I would say to myself, "What the heck are you doing?" But God is good in so many ways. Through dating his friend, God supernaturally arranged the meeting of the love of my life. Sometimes there are stepping stones placed in our path that will ultimately lead us to God's calling for our lives. For some, it is instantaneously, which I'm sure would be nice, but for others it is a step by step process to walk in the will of God. For me, it has been a process and for that, I am grateful. I have learned all that is in this book from the process of life. Death to self can be a slow walk, but the outcome is a sprint to Christ.

Continuing on slowly, year after year, I grew numb to the actual power of God. I attended church when I moved to NYC after college. I remember going each Sunday listening to the preacher, joining in worship, and thinking I was walking with Christ because I attended church. I even tried to reach out and sing on the worship team. Alas, they notified me that I may better serve the church elsewhere. For me, being a singer and musician, this was very discouraging and turned my heart a little further away from God. I was in NYC to make it big!

I sang in studio's, I rapped for some big names in the industry, yet no matter how close I got to fame, I couldn't seal the deal. Things always got in the way. Most of the time, it was due to my material. I heard things like, "It's too Godly! People don't want to hear a singer or rapper talk about Jesus." They told me that if I would just make my first album for the world to love, that after that I could do as I pleased. Then after I had a fan base, I could sing whatever my pretty heart desired. This felt so wrong to me. I couldn't wrap my mind around the fact that God was giving me amazingly poetic verses, yet no one wanted to hear them. I grew tired of the same monotonous way of life. Since the love of my life lived in Miami, when he asked me to move there so that we could be together, I said yes! I thought "Ok

God, I am ready for a new adventure, a new phase in my life!" Boy was I in for a surprise. After making living arrangements, I journeyed to Miami, Florida. I had no family there, no church, and no job, but I did have the man that I knew I was going to marry. As I settled in, I decided it was time to find a new church home. I went to several churches in many different areas of Miami, yet nothing felt like home. Nothing was sitting well in my spirit until one day I received a little flyer in the mail about a church I hadn't yet visited. I began to attend, and continued for years. Now at this point I'm sure there are some of you asking yourselves what any of this has to do with demons. I promise you, I am approaching this part of my life. So to continue, my life seemed okay. I had settled in a beautiful city with the love of my life, a good job, and a church that felt something like home to me. I had it all! Well, not exactly. I yearned for something more. I remember crying while asking God to fix my life and give me more.

About seven years passed I had a one year old daughter and a decent relationship with my love, but still I cried for more. One evening I had just finished cleaning up from dinner. Most likely I had made some Italian or Jamaican dish for my family to enjoy. Afterwards I put my daughter to bed, lit a candle, and took a hot bath. It was this evening's bed time that I remember very well. I cried "Oh God! There must be more to life than this!" And in a blink of an eye I saw myself in college, years ago. God had reminded me of my gifts that I had asked Him to take away. So right then and there, I said, "Father, please return my gifts to me! I just know I can handle them now." I then dozed off into a deep sleep. Not much changed after this, just a few more vivid dreams than usual. About a year after I said that prayer, my life began to change.

I was praying one evening and I had my first vision since I was about eleven years old. I had a vision of three old women dancing around a fire, chanting my name, and speaking some language I did not know. It seemed they were chanting a spell of some sort. I had no idea what to do with this vision, but it was so clear in my mind. So, I did what any sane human would do, I ignored it! As I carried on with my week, when something strange happened. My daughter began to cry saying that she saw a black shadow of a man walking through our house.

I immediately remembered my college days of seeing demons. On the rare occasions when I saw them, that was exactly how they appeared to me. A frightening black shadow, or a looming dark figure that seemed to be bolted to the floor would appear. At this point I began to pay close attention to what was going on around me, my daughter, and around the house. It intensified greatly. My daughter was now seeing these figures at the babysitter's house, her aunt's and her uncle's houses, but mostly in our home. I was always afraid in my home. I would walk the long hallway to get to my bedroom and in the evening after everyone was sleeping, only chills would run up my spine. I was uncomfortable sitting in my own living room.

I began to bless the house with holy water that I had retrieved from a Catholic church, hang crosses up, and pray over my home. My brother was instructing me on how to do this, but the people at my church weren't able to offer help. Everyone told me that the power of God was greater than these dark entities so I shouldn't worry. Yet, I was afraid, and constantly bothered by one spirit or another. I remember sitting on my couch watching some random sitcom when a metal cross my sister had given me as a gift began banging loudly off of my bedroom door. I muted the television, and sat frozen as I listened to the resonating sound of metal hitting off my door. There were no fans on, no windows open, and my daughter was sound asleep. I prayed quietly for God to give me courage to stand up and go look at how this cross was moving.

I stood up, shaking with fear, walking slowly over to the hallway that led to my bedroom. My heart felt like it was beating outside of my chest! My feet were so heavy, they felt like they had concrete blocks attached to them. But I repeated what my brother had told me over and over in my head, " I rebuke you spirit of fear, in the name of Jesus. I rebuke you spirit of fear, in Jesus' name!" Over and over I said this as I slowly walked to the entrance of the hallway. As I peered around the corner, I saw a 5 inch by 8 inch metal cross, violently smashing off of my bedroom door, on its own momentum. I was in disbelief really. I didn't understand why this was happening, or how this was happening; until I saw a dark gray shadow move quickly into the bathroom. While the cross was still clanging loudly, I put my hands in the air and said with serious conviction, "In the name of Jesus Christ, I rebuke you right now!!" The cross stopped immediately. No more sound, no more chills, just me standing in the hallway with my hands up, feeling like I had lost my mind. This moment was monumental for me. This moment marked the start of my race back into Jesus' arms.

I became excited, enthusiastic, and overly curious about the spirit world. I decided it was time to begin studying angels and demons. When I spoke words with conviction and they literally removed a demonic entity from my home, I felt the power of God! I liked it! I wanted to know everything I could. So I began a pursuit of building a library of books, including the Bible, of course, to soak in all I was able to attain. I was working a part time waitressing job and homeschooling my daughter, yet I felt like a full time student. Each spare moment I got, I read about demons. I read about their purpose, their strategies, their manifestations, and all of their names. I must say that when you do a study to search for things that God has put on your heart, to keep it Godly! Use Christian references and the Bible alongside of prayer and fasting. Unfortunately, I once again made a grave mistake. I began to delve into studying other religions. My intentions were genuine and true to God's call on my life, but without the sole guidance of the Holy Spirit, the sin in my life and having no accountability through other members of the body, I entered into very dangerous territory.

As I thoroughly read books on voodoo, hoodoo, sanitaria, freemasonry, and demonology, new age, physics, metaphysics, universalism, creationism, and illuminati, I developed an unhealthy obsession to know more. I was watching paranormal shows on a regular basis as well as horror movies, and I also frequently visited botanicas for supplies. I read that sage would remove evil from a place, and that burning a white candle would bring purity to my home and that carrying certain beads or stones in my bra would protect me and draw light to me. And of course, without knowing it, satan began plotting on my future. It seemed everywhere I would turn there was a new age shop to explore, or some random psychic would be at a party and come pick me out to tell me things. I have so many stories on this, that in retrospect, it was obviously satan planting his nasty seeds in my life and soul. I remember walking to the grocery store in Kingston, Jamaica when a very old, almost blind, dreaded man stopped me to give me a very important message about my life. He told me that I was a special and anointe woman and who I was going to marry. It sometimes helps to look back on things that happened in life to see the outcome years later.

I was still attending church regularly, and reading the Bible, but was I lost? Was I even aware of the path I was headed down? The answer is yes, I was lost, and no, I had no clue. I had no idea that the things I was spending my time on were in themselves a demonic act. I thought I was a good student, and that I was finally taking control of my life. As the years went on, I was continually attacked spiritually by works of voodoo and sanitaria by certain women that had personal problems with my love life. The curses and hexes were regularly coming my way. I would often have visions of certain people putting pictures of me and my loved ones in the center of a sacrificed chicken to be buried until rotting. I knew their hate for me was dark and evil, and although those I loved may have believed what I told them, they also thought that God would simply protect me. If I was perfect and without sin, I would have been protected and this would have been accurate, however, I was not, hence giving satan a foothold to move in my life.

They often attacked my love life, but sometimes just for fun they would attack my job or my friendships. I began to get excited. I was growing with power, and understanding. I enjoyed getting rid of these things when they were sent to me. I enjoyed lighting candles knowing it was defeating them. And then one day, I decided to go to a shaman to hear about my awesome life, when he told me that someone had put a spirit of death upon me. I was not shocked at all, but boy was I scared. He said he could remove it with a very expensive cleansing, and a ritual of some sort. I left wondering what had all this come to? My love life was a mess, my days were filled with fear and torment, and now there was someone trying to kill me? What was I to do?

I remember wondering if God would do this to me? Would God put me in this position? I lived the next six months or so in complete fear that I was going to die. I worried for my daughter, her father, and my family. I was at my wits end. I could take no more of this. People hiring people to send demons and allowing myself to get entangled in to the demonic supernatural world was just some crazy movie I was in. "This must be a dream!" I would say to myself. It was a living nightmare! It was getting in the way of my love relationship, it was scaring the life out of my daughter and I, and it was making my friends and family think I was a little crazy. I did the only thing I knew how to do at this point, I learned how to read tarot cards and began meditating. I meditated for hours a day. I would lock myself in my bedroom and lay there, motionless, waiting for some type of cosmic event that would change my life. I studied metaphysics, and philosophies about quantum physics. I memorized mantras stemming from the nations of India and Africa. I became smarter. I became stronger. I would walk through a mall and hear a voice tell me that that man over there was cheating on his wife, or that that woman's brother died in a car accident. I knew this was it. This was good. This was true power.

Behind the scenes there were great powers of both good and evil fighting for me. It is all in retrospect that I can now speak with wisdom on this time in my life. I am going to fill you in on the truth of the matter in a few moments. So as I moved in this power, I had friends asking me about their future and my answers were always right. I had others ask me to read their tarot cards because my answers were always right. Who wouldn't want to know their future? Who wouldn't want to know if their husband or wife was cheating? It got to the point where I was so accurate in that which I would say, that it became even a bit overwhelming to me when I would see what my loved ones were doing 10 miles away. I would venture out for a much needed girls night out, when at some point in the evening it would strike. The words coming from wherever, would come upon me. So eventually I began to speak to people of their problems. I remember sitting at a bar where my dear friend was bartending, and a man coming up to me. He reached out his hand to shake mine, and all of the sudden I heard that he was going through a divorce because his wife had cheated on him. So this time, I decided to take it outside my friends circle and try a random person. As I told him this, he broke down crying. He broke down so violently that the manager asked us to go outside. I couldn't believe it. How powerful I felt. So when this worked out so well, I decided to continue. It seemed that it was most accurate and powerful when the person would touch me. When they would shake my hand, or touch my shoulder, I would hear all different kinds of information about them. So one evening, I met with a friend to do a card reading. I came with all necessary tools. Cards, sage, and crystals. This is where it got weird. Typically when I would read someone's cards, I would have them shuffle, putting their energy on them. So after this I would burn sage as to clear the area and the person of any interference in the supernatural world.

I began to flip the cards as she asked questions about her personal life. I flipped the first card, the second card, and by the third card, I heard the name "Thomas." I continued with the flipping of cards. Each time I would flip a card, I would hear the name Thomas in my right ear. It got to the point where it was annoying me. I thought, "who the heck is Thomas and why do I keep hearing this name?" Finally I blurted out, "WHO IS THOMAS?" The girl began to cry. Thomas was her deceased father. So as I sat there wondering why I was hearing about her dead father, he showed up! He, meaning her dead father! Floating in the air, just above her head, was her dead father, Thomas. He began to speak very loudly and with persistence. He gave messages for both she and her mother, very personal, very accurate messages. Even though this was the first time a dead man had ever shown up and given me messages for someone, I was definitely out of my element. The meeting seemed to bring much healing to her and her mother. It seemed to set them free from concerns they had, and comfort in knowing he was there with them. The next day, she thanked me over and over, as she felt freer somehow. I was at home wondering why I was seeing dead people now. I was ok with hearing accurate words, and I was ok with seeing things in my mind, but I was not ok with seeing glowing dead men floating above people's heads telling me what to say! I pondered for hours about this. The same thing continually came to my mind. It was a story that I remembered in the Bible. It was part of the story of Saul. 1 Samuel 28:1-25 (NIV):

> ***In those days the Philistines gathered their forces to fight against Israel. Achish said to David, "You must understand that you and your men will accompany me in the army." David said, "Then you will see for yourself what your servant can do." Achish replied,***

"Very well, I will make you my bodyguard for life." Now Samuel was dead, and all Israel had mourned for him and buried him in his own town of Ramah. Saul had expelled the mediums and spiritists from the land. The Philistines assembled and came and set up camp at Shunem, while Saul gathered all Israel and set up camp at Gilboa. When Saul saw the Philistine army, he was afraid; terror filled his heart. He inquired of the Lord, but the Lord did not answer him by dreams or Urim or prophets. Saul then said to his attendants, "Find me a woman who is a medium, so I may go and inquire of her." "There is one in Endor," they said. So Saul disguised himself, putting on other clothes, and at night he and two men went to the woman. "Consult a spirit for me," he said, "and bring up for me the one I name." But the woman said to him, "Surely you know what Saul has done. He has cut off the mediums and spiritists from the land. Why have you set a trap for my life to bring about my death?" Saul swore to her by the LORD, "As surely as the Lord lives, you will not be punished for this." Then the woman asked, "Whom shall I bring up for you?" "Bring up Samuel," he said. When the woman saw Samuel, she cried out at the top of her voice and said to Saul, "Why have you deceived me? You are Saul!" The king said to her, "Don't be afraid. What do you see?" The

woman said, "I see a ghostly figure coming up out of the earth." "What does he look like?" he asked. "An old man wearing a robe is coming up," she said. Then Saul knew it was Samuel, and he bowed down and prostrated himself with his face to the ground. Samuel said to Saul, "Why have you disturbed me by bringing me up?"

"I am in great distress," Saul said. "The Philistines are fighting against me, and God has departed from me. He no longer answers me, either by prophets or by dreams. So I have called on you to tell me what to do." Samuel said, "Why do you consult me, now that the LORD has departed from you and become your enemy? The LORD has done what he predicted through me. The LORD has torn the kingdom out of your hands and given it to one of your neighbors—to David. Because you did not obey the LORD or carry out his fierce wrath against the Amalekites, the LORD has done this to you today. The LORD will deliver both Israel and you into the hands of the Philistines, and tomorrow you and your sons will be with me. The LORD will also give the army of Israel into the hands of the Philistines."

Immediately Saul fell full length on the ground, filled with fear because of Samuel's words. His strength was gone, for he had eaten nothing all that day and all that night.

When the woman came to Saul and saw that he was greatly shaken, she said, "Look, your servant has obeyed you. I took my life in my hands and did what you told me to do. Now please listen to your servant and let me give you some food so you may eat and have the strength to go on your way." He refused and said, "I will not eat." But his men joined the woman in urging him, and he listened to them. He got up from the ground and sat on the couch. The woman had a fattened calf at the house, which she butchered at once. She took some flour, kneaded it and baked bread without yeast. Then she set it before Saul and his men, and they ate. That same night they got up and left.

After reading this scripture over again, I was even more confused. I was then led to the book of Deuteronomy 18:10-12 (NASB):

"There shall not be found among you anyone who makes his son or his daughter pass through the fire, one who uses divination, one who practices witchcraft, or one who interprets omens, or a sorcerer, or one who casts a spell, or a medium, or a spiritist, or one who calls up the dead. For whoever does these things is detestable to the LORD; and because of these detestable things the LORD your God will drive them out before you."

Wait a second here! You mean what happened with my friend's dead father is detestable to the Lord? I realize from a worldly perspective this must have seemed fine. It wasn't fine to me. God began to tug at my heart about what was happening in my life. It was a very distinct difference from the feelings or words I would receive otherwise. This was the conviction of the Holy Spirit of God himself. I sought out help. I went to church, and spoke with some people there about all that was going on in my life. I was scared. I was so scared that all I had been doing was an abomination to God. I feared hell. I feared my life would get worse. But as my church folk directed me, they said "well, Saul spoke to the dead in the Bible, so I'm sure it is ok." As we further discussed all the other things that were going on in my life, I was still very unsettled. It was as if God were putting a blanket of wisdom over me. It was so heavy that I couldn't bear it at times. I thought to myself more than once that I was on the wrong path. I decided to really seek for answers. This was much bigger than me. This was the King of Kings, Lord of Lords speaking to me now. I took it very seriously as I dove into further study. I read, and I prayed and I searched out Christian books. I came across a minister of God via the internet. Some of you may have heard of him, as he is very well known in the Christian world. His name is Derek Prince. Although he is now dead, his teachings were readily available on YouTube.

I listened to Derek for hours and hours, day after day. I received prayer after the lessons were over and felt things leaving me, and I felt God healing me. I began to hear a voice that I hadn't heard in a while. It was Jesus. After one of the lessons concerning things in our homes that attract demons, I began to throw everything away. I threw away my tarot cards first, then all the new age stones, then all of my African masks that lined the walls of my home. I threw away all sage, and all books dealing with anything new age, witchcraft, or voodoo. I cried out to the Lord for many weeks, repenting for what I had done.

I asked that He would spare me because I didn't completely understand what I was doing. Yet I also took responsibility for the things I did know I was doing that were against Hm. I held responsibility in it all. As I studied, I came across a prayer. It was a prayer to remove demons from me. I thought about it and thought about it some more, until I could think no more. I thought "Do I have demons? I can't see them on me if I do! Is it even possible for a Christian to have a demon? How would God allow that? Why was I being led to this prayer?" My mind went round and round like a merry go round, but after many hours of deliberation, I decided to do it. What harm could it do, right? It certainly couldn't hurt. I mean after all, it was a prayer to Jesus. As I began to repeat the words aloud that were on the screen, I felt the need to raise my hands up, in honor of God's grace and redemption. I had them raised as high as they would go. I spoke the words with meaning and assertion. As I continued, my hand got a strange sensation. They began to tingle with electricity. It felt similar to a limb when it falls asleep. The tingle was getting more and more intense as I declared these demons to leave me. By the end of the prayer it felt like that of an electric jolt. It was amazing. Definitely a strange feeling and a mystery to me. At the end of the prayer I was to say Amen and just breathe. No more praying. No praying in tongues, no praying at all. I was just to breathe deeply. In and out I felt air slowly leave my lungs, and within about 30 seconds, the strangest thing happened.

I began to cough! I coughed and coughed for over 5 minutes at least. It felt as if some type of chemical or acid was in my throat and my body was expelling it. Hands still on fire, I made my way to the toilet. I thought for sure I was going to vomit. As I kneeled there on the floor, face in the toilette bowl, I remember thinking, "What the heck is happening here? Is this normal? Is this what releasing a demon feels like? Am I sick? Did I get the flu somehow?" Needless to say, I was confused and a bit mystified by the whole experience. But just as I thought this cannot get any worse, I begin to throw up. But nothing was coming out.. I was dry-heaving into an empty toilet. It finally ceased, and I wiped my mouth with some toilet paper, thanking God that it had come to an end. When I threw the bunch of wadded up paper in the toilette, it was a dark grey color. I got scared and jumped up to look in the mirror. Nothing was there. My mouth looked normal. My gums and tongue were pink. I looked in the toilette again thinking I must have been seeing things, but it was still there, a wadded up ball of grey toilet paper in my toilet. I walked into my bedroom dumbfounded with this new experience. I was confused, yet light. I was feeling strange, yet full. So after this event, I was to pray that the Holy Spirit would fill all wounds left in my soul from any demons that may have left me. As I did this, the most powerful, electrifying moment that I had ever experienced in my walk with Christ so far occurred. It was so overwhelming I fell straight to the floor and wept. I cried and laughed hysterically. The transition from one emotion to the next was so quick that I, again, was in unknown territory. But this time, it was the best confusion I had ever felt. I was free! I was in a whirlwind tunnel of the Holy Spirit of the Almighty God himself! It was as if I was a tree, great in size that had been uprooted by an enormous tornado, only to be placed in a lush ground full of water and sunshine. It was exhilarating. One of the best moments of my life even to this day.

After this interestingly, beautiful experience, I was famished. I was so hungry, I went to the kitchen to prepare a meal for myself. I saw the Appleton rum sitting there on the counter, and thought what a great time to have a drink. I was a social drinker at best, and occasionally I enjoyed having a drink while I prepared dinner for my family. The thought of having the drink this night, however, passed quickly. I decided after all that I didn't want one. Then the next night passed, and the following night too. A week had passed and for some reason, I still didn't want an alcoholic beverage. I thought to myself that it was a bit strange for me, yet I went with it. Something would stop me each time I thought of having a drink. So I brushed it off and decided I was going out with my girlfriends. I said to myself, " I will have a drink at dinner with the girls when we're out." However, I found myself turning down drinks while out as well. It seemed to me that God had removed a demon affiliated with my drinking habits. I wouldn't say that I had a drinking problem, but perhaps it was headed that way. I don't really know, and to be honest, I don't really care. All I know is that Jesus took something out of me that made me want to drink. It has been years since I have had even a sip of alcohol. I want to make it clear here that I have no judgment on anyone, Christian or not, for their choices with alcohol. This is my story, and I am sharing how God has moved in my life. That is all.

After this event, I noticed so many things changing

constantly. Things began to change in me. I heard God speaking to me. My friends would ask me to "look." This meant they wanted me to speak about what I would hear or see in their lives; perhaps a circumstance in their lives. But it just didn't work like that anymore. I couldn't just look and see what was happening. I had to pray and ask. Sometimes God would tell me, and sometimes He wouldn't. My hours of meditation and operating my third eye, turned into hours of worship and prayer, or meditating on the Word of God and scripture. My life was changing and it was powerful too. It was a different kind of powerful however. It was the power of God that was in me, not the power of "God knows what," in me! I did wonder what going out with my girlfriends would be like after this. So I thought I had better give it a go. I prayed in tongues the whole drive there. A little nervous, yet excited to see what God would do. He did NOT disappoint!

It started at dinner with a girlfriend. I was hearing words for people. I would look at them and hear God speak about their struggles, and also what He had planned for their lives. Then off we went to a club. The moment I entered the club I saw darkness in the air, but I also saw lights above people's heads. They looked like candles lit in a dark room. I spoke to those people because I felt as though the Lord was showing me that they knew Him. In the whole club, I saw three people with the light. I spoke to one about his wife that was trying to divorce him. I instructed Him on how to begin healing his marriage, as that is what God desired. He received it well. The word was very accurate, so he would have been crazy not to. Then I made my way to the next man. He was at a table with many people. I spoke to him about having a business that God wanted to bless because of his prayers. He was so shocked that he rounded up his friends and asked who had been talking to me about him. After a lot of laughing, I explained that Jesus was giving me this message for him. He, too, received it well. At this point I was feeling good! I was obeying God. I was hearing God. It felt like home somehow. A comfort came upon me and made me feel like I was finally fulfilling my purpose. I looked up to find the third person but she was gone. So we decided to move on to the next stop. At this point I didn't even care where we were going, I was just walking in a zone straight to Jesus.

We left, and my friends needed to stop close by to get something from the store. I believe it was cigarettes. As I stood outside alone waiting for them, I looked to my right and saw a homeless man trying to get money for the bus. I said "Father, if you want me to help him, send him over to me." Before I could blink, he approached me for some cash to catch the bus. I apologized saying that I had no cash, but I could pray for him. He graciously accepted my offer. So outside the club, in front of all the sexy people waiting in line trying to get in, I laid my hand on his shoulder, bowed my head, and prayed. God gave me a word for him that there was something wrong with the left side of his brain. He then cried and explained that when he was a boy, no older than two or three, that his father would beat him on that side of his head! With a bat! I got quite emotional myself, but wanted to stay focused so Jesus could do what He wanted for this man. At this time, my friends were coming out of the store watching and waiting for me to finish. I prayed for healing in his brain, skull, and soul. I was there for about 10 minutes praying for him. I thought, how nice it was, and hoped I obeyed God. When I caught up to my friends, they told me that while

I was praying, his eyes changed color. They said they were brown, then turned blue, then back to brown. This made me very happy, as I knew God had touched this man's life!

I am not able to continue to relate all of the beautiful adventures God has sent me on because this book would be too long. However, I will tell you that after months of this, A production company caught wind of what I was doing on South beach and offered me a contract to film a show on it. I contemplated this for over a month, as I wanted to spread what Jesus could do, on a national level, but alas there was a problem. It seemed like when I was pursuing my music and no one wanted to sign me for my biblically inspired music. They wanted to call me a psychic and I, of course, had a problem with this, as I was not a psychic. They also said, in order for it to be shopped to the larger, mainstream networks, I wouldn't be able to say the name Jesus. Hmmmm, it was a no brainer; for it was Jesus that was doing everything. I was simply a vessel for him to use.

Shortly after this, I was praying for a new church to attend. I felt deeply that God wanted me to move on from my church, but didn't know where. I prayed and prayed, when one day, I heard the name of a church. I quickly grabbed my phone to look it up. I called the phone number and spoke to the senior pastor of the church. He was gracious and loving. I told him a bit of my story explaining the need for a church that moves freely in the Holy Spirit. I had been confined long enough and wanted to share what I had experienced at home in my room, on a larger scale. I knew it was possible because many years before when I had attended my brother's church, I spoke in tongues for the first time. He assured me that they allowed the movement of the Holy Spirit at their church. But then I was interrupted. I heard God say the name "Cathy" while I was on the phone. I didn't want to say anything to him because of how it may sound, but God spoke it again. Out of obedience, I said to him "Who is Cathy?" He replied, "That's my wife!" It was then that I knew I must attend this church, and I have called it home ever since.

As time went on, I continued to hear the Lord in all I did. I tried to obey in everything and do all I could to please Him. He again continued to put the supernatural world of demons and angels on my heart. Within these years of study, He began to expose satan's plan even more. I would like to take some time now in the breaking down of the structure of the kingdom of darkness. Let us refer now to Matthew 12:26 and 28 (KJV):

> ***And if satan cast out satan, he is divided against himself; how shall then his kingdom stand? But if I cast out devils by the Spirit of God, then the kingdom of God is come unto you.***

Jesus clearly states here that there are two prevalent kingdoms. Satan has a kingdom, but so does God. Referring now back to the scripture in Ephesians 6:12 (NKJV):

> ***For we do not wrestle against flesh and blood, but against principalities, against powers, against the rulers of the darkness of this age, against spiritual hosts of wickedness in the heavenly places.***

To break this down, we must look again at the fact

that we do not fight against human beings, but rather against secret satanic powers in the invisible realm. In his Kingdom, there is a hierarchy of structure just like that of God. Lucifer was perfect to God in his ways from the time of his creation to the time of his rebellion. He was a master of worship and music in heaven. He shown brilliantly with jewels in heaven. In Ezekiel 28: 14 (KJV) it speaks of him as an ***anointed cherub that covereth.*** What was it that he covered? He covered the very throne of God that all cherub angels covered. He had a very high seating in the kingdom of God. There are two reasons I'm explaining this; the first is because we must understand that satan is wise and was once held in God's hand as anointed. Secondly, understand that since he held such a high seat in heaven and held great power that this was his motivation not only to rebel, but also to use as a construct of his own kingdom. The sin that caused Lucifer to fall was that of pride. His beauty was great, his power was great, and because of his rebellion in pride, his fall was great. He was a leader; convincing one-third of the angels in heaven to follow him in rebellion. Could this be the reason that more than half of our world falls to the deceit of satan? Is he using his leadership skills on us? I believe the answer to that is a definitive yes! Amongst many other tactics, satan draws people in to worshipping him without even being aware. Are some of us being used as puppets on a string? Absolutely! I strongly feel that the sin of pride is a sin that has taken over not only the unchurched but also the churched.

There is a bit of controversy when discussing whether or not Christians can be demon possessed or not. From a personal perspective, I know that demons can and do live inside of a human being. I watch them leave every time Jesus delivers a person from a demon. However, it is not scriptural that a sincere, spirit-filled, born-again, person can be possessed by the devil. Let's take a look at Mark 1:21-28 (NKJV):

> *Then they went into Capernaum, and immediately on the Sabbath He entered the synagogue and taught. And they were astonished at His teaching, for He taught them as one having authority, and not as the scribes. Now there was a man in their synagogue with an unclean spirit. And he cried out, saying, "Let us alone! What have we to do with You, Jesus of Nazareth? Did You come to destroy us? I know who You are—the Holy One of God!" But Jesus rebuked him, saying, "Be quiet, and come out of him!" And when the unclean spirit had convulsed him and cried out with a loud voice, he came out of him. Then they were all amazed, so that they questioned among themselves, saying, "What is this? What new doctrine is this? For with authority He commands even the unclean spirits, and they obey Him." And immediately His fame spread throughout all the region around Galilee."*

First, let's acknowledge that Jesus was in a synagogue with "holy" people, under the Law of Moses. Yes, they were Jewish and not yet Christian, however, Christianity didn't yet exist. As we break this down, it would be a fair comparison to look at these "holy" people as we look at today's church. He was teaching on the importance of having and using authority when a man with an unclean spirit spoke. I have noticed in my life also this is true. Anytime I take and use my authority in Jesus, over any part of the demonic realm, an unclean spirit will raise his nasty head. As I walk as Jesus did, I also try to do as Jesus did. When the unclean spirit cried out, Jesus rebuked him and said ***"Be quiet and come out of him."*** There are a few things we need to look at here. "Be quiet," translates in the Greek to "Be muzzled." I tell you this in hopes that you just received a mental picture of a vicious creature being muzzled immediately. So this thing had to first shut up, and then come out. It works the same way for any spirit-filled Christian. He must first discern that an unclean spirit is causing the problem, tell it so be silenced, and finally, cast it out. Because the living Spirit of Jesus dwells within us, we too can do just that. My second point here is that demons can and do torment Christians. If there is one thing that I have learned in my walk with Christ, is this. Please don't be offended, but there is not one human being that I know, that doesn't have more than one demon influencing them. However, if you learn the tools that I am implementing in this book, you can always, not only get rid of them, but make sure the same ones do not return. It is not an easy thing to do because we are the sons of Adam and we will always sin, but it is possible to keep these things in check on a constant basis.

The first satanic hierarchy in Ephesians 6:12 speaks of "principalities." They are also known as the "Prince" which many scriptures point to. These creatures rule over nations. On the earthly side of things, you will see all types of demonic oppression. Starvation, murder, domination through socialism or communism, and for that matter, all negative saddening things that happen in different nations are subject to a Principality. The suffering of that nation is the actual assignment of the Prince of the air.

Next, there is a lesser order that dominates over a

particular city in that nation. If you pray and ask God what order is dominating a city, you will most likely get an answer that a very strong principality in the hierarchy of satan's kingdom is the culprit. Moving on from here, Ephesians speaks about "powers." These are in the kingdom, yet a step down from the princes. They take control over human beings. These are the demon creatures that I see on people, and also the creatures I see leaving people when commanded out in the name of Jesus. They can influence humans to do any sort of demonic act, depending on our agreement with them, or keep us blinded from moving forward in our relationship with God. For example, when someone is openly having sex outside of marriage, they are openly coming into agreement with perverse, seducing spirits that want us to be outside the gates Their purpose is to deceive us so well, separating us from God. We become blind, forming hardened hearts, and eventually given over to a completely depraved mind.

It is also important to discuss hate. Hate is shown in numerous ways, causing multiple disastrous affects. What lies behind this thought, action, or emotion, is usually the spirit of death. Soon, I will go much further into detail about specific cause and effect strategy satan uses with his demons.

Next in the scripture, is the power of the "rulers of darkness." In the Greek, this means world rulers. They are normally influencing people in the ways of false religion, and falling into the deceptions of witchcraft. This is for the non-Christian, as well as the Christian. For the non-Christian, this is why they are in fact, non. While for the believer, it leads people away from the true teaching of Jesus, thus becoming rebellious in many ways. Witchcraft can be used interchangeably as a generic term for that of pride and rebellion. There are different facets of this spirit, yes, but the root of the problem is pride and rebellion. This is even the case when witchcraft becomes a verb and is used in the form of voodoo, hoodoo, wicca, or santeria. It matters not, because in each of these religions or ways of life, they are rebelling from the will of the living God; knowingly or not.

Lastly, let's discuss "spiritual hosts of wickedness in heavenly realms." Wickedness is a power that intervenes with God's perfect plan in people's lives. The horrible things that can happen here on earth, which I'm sure the majority of you have experienced, can be from spiritual hosts of wickedness. Premature death or death before God's appointed time is that of wickedness. Committing suicide and random accidents that take someone's life, are all due to the power of wickedness. We must put on the full armor of God, each day, sometimes a few times a day, to resist this power of wickedness that takes so many before the time God has intended. When God gave satan authority over the earth, satan took and used his authority. We must be wise people and do as God instructed us in order to survive that which satan has authority over. Jesus already won! This means that when we step into that which He has promised his people, we will be protected from satan's destruction upon our lives; hence the Kingdom of God principle. But, we hold responsibility in knowing how, and then following through with action. God made us an intelligent species so that we could glorify Him. We must do our part. Take a look at this story.

I just can't begin to express the importance of understanding how these powers are at work and will push relentlessly until we use our authority in Christ to stop them. This is a story that is happening right now as

I am writing. About two days ago, I was at home writing. I had one hour to write before going to a Chris Tomlin concert. I was blessed with backstage passes that enabled me to meet some of the amazing people on tour. As I went to save what I considered one precious hour of supernatural writing, my computer began to glitch. It glitched so much, and so quickly that my computer shut down before I could save any of the information I had typed. I got angry at satan because I knew with this chapter in particular that would interfere. How did I know? First of all, I am divulging secret information God has given me, hopefully exposing his agenda. So logically, I knew something would happen. He does not like to be exposed, as it gives that with authority the power to triumph the same way Jesus did. Secondly, before starting the chapter, I cried. I couldn't stomach even having to write about satan or his evil. I dreaded even beginning this chapter, but in obedience to God I must, and I knew I must. So now, two days later after praying for massive protection over myself, family and my computer, I decided it was a good day to do some writing at a coffee shop.

As I sat and prayed and contemplated the information God wanted me to share, I felt a severe change in the atmosphere. I began to get light headed, dizzy, and confused. I felt anxiety creeping into my skin. I recognize each and every one of these signs. It was a direct hit by satan himself. I knew it all too well, as I have dealt with each of these independently in my walk with Jesus. So after noticing the change in atmosphere, I calmly sat back and observed my surroundings as I prayed. I saw a woman in orange ordering her coffee when God said, "She is a witch and was sent here for you." So I immediately thanked him, and took authority over any power she may have held. It improved for a few minutes until she and her counterpart decided to sit directly across from me at my table. The feelings of death and anxiety, dizziness and repulsion swept over me like a tidal wave. So much so that I stood up to go pray aloud in the bathroom and almost fell over. Not able to walk straight, knocking into the walls, I struggled to make it to the bathroom. As I entered the bathroom, it got worse. Being in a confined area with such evil is never fun. Now it was here that God told me she was sent simply to get me to fear my life, go home, and stop writing. It was so powerful that this notion definitely had crossed my mind a few times. But thanks to my Lord and savior, Jesus, I was able to rebuke all of the witch's demons, their agendas and their purposes for keeping me from writing. I took authority and I rebuked all that Jesus had told me. I walked out of the bathroom still with a bit of dizziness. I sat down and began to literally blow the Holy Spirit from my mouth upon this woman. Within 30 seconds, she stood up, looked around, and left. I went outside to sit for a moment and pray over myself. I also asked the Holy Spirit to come and fill the place. This is just one example of the way that satan will interfere with doing God's work when we are being obedient to our calling. So with that, I encourage all of you to be more sensitive to His spirit and that which is happening around you as you live out your purpose!

I will have to continue to use His great authority in my life in order to survive. Thank God I have this option. Thank God He is already preparing me and my family with information for the end times and to pray in advance for what we will need. I'm going to take this opportune time to reveal a prophetic dream that God gave me almost exactly a year ago to this day. He did however bring up the necessity in my heart to put this dream in this book. I call it a prophetic prediction. Often times, when God gives dreams that stay vivid even as time passes, they are very important. These dreams in particular were in two parts, two nights in a row.

The first dream was of me in a large factory. I was walking around on the metal catwalks that were about 100ft off the ground. As I walked slowly around this dark factory, a loud voice that sounded like a trumpet, spoke to me. I knew immediately this voice was God's, and I stopped walking and turned my head toward the sky. He said something very bold. He said something very significant. God said "Get everyone off South Beach Thursday the 11th." After He spoke these words, I woke up. But I didn't just wake up and go back to sleep, I woke up suddenly and sat up with a great conviction to pray for Miami. I was shaken and sad. Eventually, I fell back asleep and my day continued as normal, except that this dream had gripped my thoughts and spirit. The following night when it was time to sleep, I remember it being a bit difficult to fall asleep. I felt a great responsibility already with the dream I had the night before. How would I get everyone off of South Beach? Why would God tell me something I had no power to change? Regardless, I had to sleep at some point, right? Eventually I dozed off when I received my second prophetic dream concerning Miami. In this dream I was in my spirit body hovering over the shore of Miami Beach from an aerial view, and as I scanned over the sea shore with my eyes, I saw hundreds of thousands of dead bodies lining the coastline. There on the sand, lying motionless were so many dead people. Then I was awakened with the same heavy heart. I began to question God and ask Him when it was going to happen, how it was going to happen, and how I could possible tell everyone in Miami to get off South Beach. I went to church and decided to ask a few of my prophetic friends for their help. They all said to pray about it and that sometimes, because God is our friend, He shares things with us, to grieve or celebrate with Him, but not to actually do anything about it. So I did just that. I continued to pray and ask God to open a door, if He, in fact, wanted me to share with South Beach that they need to evacuate on Thursday the 11th. I got no answer in return. Nothing was said again until almost exactly one year to the day of these dreams. God told me to put this word in this book and that will be the way that I notify so many people. So there it is. As of right now, I do not know what year or month He was speaking of, but I do know it is something that will wipe out much of Florida and that it will happen on Thursday the 11th. I also know that He brought it up almost a year later for a reason, so take head to this word my friends. Begin to pray and ask God for guidance Will you ask for God to open your supernatural senses so that you too can fight? All we have to do is give Jesus permission, follow through with His instructions, and watch satan flee.

7 DEMONS

I would love to say that this chapter is a chapter that I was looking forward to writing, however, I highly dislike giving any of satan's soldiers credit or validation of any sort. I felt God's guidance to write this chapter due to the importance for the reader to gain knowledge of their adversary. Unbelievably, demonology once played a huge role in my walk with Christ. It wasn't just about knowing their names, their functions, or their agenda's, but also the journey of getting to know Jesus through the search. It was a suggestive push from God that allowed me to delve into understanding this part of scripture and doctrine. From previous chapters, I'm sure you remember the way satan used the supernatural and the occult to seduce me away from the truth of the Lord, but there was a point when He said it was enough! Because of all the experience I had in the satanic supernatural, God will use this knowledge to teach His people the Holy supernatural. Did that mean that satan was done with the pursuit of taking my life from me? Of course not. He just found other ways to harass me. But, because I have such a close relationship with my Father, he is unable to break our union. I am grateful for my past, present and future. I am confident that Jesus knows exactly what He is doing with my life and I give Him full permission to do as He wills.

Having said that, let us jump right into the creatures that work for satan himself. Some people use the terms fallen angels and demons interchangeably, but in my opinion they are two very different beings. The fallen angels we have discussed in some detail in previous chapters when I touched upon the Nephilim and also Lucifer falling from heaven with one-third of the angels, are an important part of this satanic realm. One of the reasons this is even a debated topic is due to the book of Enoch which is great to read as an historical book, however it did not make it into the canonized Bible. Left in a place of possibility, yet it was not recognized as divine word breathed from God the creator, hence it leaves all biblical information as truth, and other non-canonical writings only as possible truth. With that in mind, Enoch spoke of demons in this way. Chapter XV (Enoch 15:8-12):

> And now, the giants, who are produced from the spirits and flesh, shall be called evil spirits upon the earth, and on the earth shall be their dwelling. Evil spirits have proceeded from their bodies; because they are born from men and from the holy Watchers is their beginning and primal origin; they shall be evil spirits on earth, and evil spirits shall they be called. [As for the spirits of heaven, in heaven shall be their dwelling, but as for the spirits of the earth which were born upon the earth, on the earth shall be their dwelling.] And the spirits of the giants afflict, oppress, destroy, attack, do battle, and work destruction on the earth, and cause trouble: they take no food, but nevertheless hunger and thirst, and cause offences. And these spirits shall rise up against the children of men and against the women, because they have proceeded from them.

The book of Enoch continues to be used as a reference to many biblical scholars, not necessarily in whole or as a complete truth, but simply as a point of reference. We can look at the angels mentioned in the bible to get an idea of the physical and personal characteristics of the angels that fell. They were once all the same. It wasn't until they joined Lucifer that they developed differing evil characteristics. To recapitulate for a moment what the Bible tells us; fallen angels have the ability to make babies with humans.

> ***That the sons of God saw the daughters of men that they were fair; and they took them wives of all which they chose. And the Lord said, My spirit shall not always strive with man, for that he also is flesh: yet his days shall be an hundred and twenty years. There were giants in the earth in those days; and also after that, when the sons of God came in unto the daughters of men, and they bare children to them, the same became mighty men which were of old, men of renown. And God saw that the wickedness of man was great in the earth, and that every imagination of the thoughts of his heart was only evil continually. And it repented the Lord that he had made man on the earth, and it grieved him at his heart.***
> Genesis 6:2-6 (KJV).

They have the ability to transform themselves into ministers of light according to 2 Corinthians 11:13-15 (KJV):

> *For such are false apostles, deceitful workers, transforming themselves into the apostles of Christ. And no marvel; for satan himself is transformed into an angel of light. Therefore it is no great thing if his ministers also be transformed as the ministers of righteousness; whose end shall be according to their works.*

They also have the ability to roam the earth looking for those to devour and also speak to God making accusations against us, according to Revelations 12:10. Let us also refer to Job 1:6-7 (KJV):

> *Now there was a day when the sons of God came to present themselves before the LORD, and satan came also among them. And the LORD said unto satan, Whence comest thou? Then satan answered the LORD, and said, From going to and fro in the earth, and from walking up and down in it.*

They have wings and are able to fly. Daniel 9:21 (KJV) states:

> *Yea, whiles I was speaking in prayer, even the man Gabriel, whom I had seen in the vision at the beginning, being caused to fly swiftly, touched me about the time of the evening oblation.*

It is very clear that fallen angels have bodies of their own, are able to fly, and we can safely assume they have wings based on the references of seraphim and their many wings. Biblically, unclean spirits and demons are used interchangeably, while fallen angels and demons are not. Satan, who is the master over every fallen angel and demon, is a counterfeit copy of that of God the Father, being Lord over all the angels. Demons are evil spirits that have no place to call home. They desperately crave to embody a person so that they don't have to walk through dry places. This is a point that is clearly made a couple times in scripture. Demons have lusts that can only be gratified and fulfilled when in a body. They themselves can only cause a basic or superficial problem when they have a body to do their bidding. I strongly feel that this is why so many people, both saved and unsaved, are in the darkness. So many people are being tormented in ways that can be overcome with a repentant heart, with some knowledge, and the ministering of the Holy Spirit. Later we will discuss the importance of casting out these spirits when in the correct spiritual state, like that of salvation, thus bringing this book to a full head. Preparation for the end times is necessary for battle. But for now, I think it is important to refer to some scripture on the demons that Jesus dealt with to gain a better understanding of why Jesus did these things.

Demons have personalities. Each of them carry a specific deed and desire that they must attain. They are everywhere; just waiting to proceed through an open door. The door, meaning an entry way, into your soul. Matthew 12:43 (KJV) ***When the unclean spirit is gone out of a man, he walketh through dry places, seeking rest, and findeth none.***

They cannot, and do not rest until they have a place to call home. This is mostly that of a human body, however, there are times where they will inhabit animals if instructed or if given no other choice. This brings me to my first example of Jesus casting out not only one demon, but many demons, in one man. You will read in a moment that the demonized man had something called a "Legion" inside of him. This translates to an army of 6000 soldiers. This is the story of the Gerasene demoniac in Mark 5:1-19 (PHILLIPS):

Jesus meets a violent lunatic

So they arrived on the other side of the lake in the country of the Gerasenes. As Jesus was getting out of the boat, a man in the grip of an evil spirit rushed to meet him from among the tombs where he was living. It was no longer possible for any human being to restrain him even with a chain. Indeed he had frequently been secured with fetters and lengths of chain, but he had simply snapped the chains and broken the fetters in pieces. No one could do anything with him. All through the night as well as in the day-time he screamed among the tombs and on the hill-side, and cut himself with stones. Now, as soon as he saw Jesus in the distance, he ran and knelt before him, yelling at the top of his voice, "What have you got to do with me, Jesus, Son of the most- high God? For God's sake, don't torture me!" For Jesus had already said, "Come out of this man, you evil spirit!" Then he asked him, "What is your name?" "My name is legion," he replied, "for there are many of us." Then he begged and prayed him not to send "them" out of the country. A large herd of pigs

was grazing there on the hill-side, and the evil spirits implored him, "Send us over to the pigs and we'll get into them!"

So Jesus allowed them to do this, and they came out of the man, and made off and went into the pigs. The whole herd of about two thousand stampeded down the cliff into the lake and was drowned. The swineherds took to their heels and spread their story in the city and all over the countryside. Then the people came to see what had happened. As they approached Jesus, they saw the man who had been devil-possessed sitting there properly clothed and perfectly sane—the same man who had been possessed by "legion"—and they were really frightened. Those who had seen the incident told them what had happened to the devil-possessed man and about the disaster to the pigs. Then they began to implore Jesus to leave their district." As he was embarking on the small boat, the man who had been possessed begged that he might go with him. But Jesus would not allow this. "Go home to your own people," he told him, "And tell them what the Lord has done for you, and how kind he has been to you!"

This story alone teaches us so much about Jesus, humans, and demons. Isn't it interesting that this legion of demons wanted desperately to stay in the country? Also that they wanted desperately to be cast into 2,000 pigs instead of on the earth to walk through dry places as referred to before in Matthew 12:43. Demons have a strong will, my friends, and having a strong will is a characteristic of a personality. Also, let us make a note here that a human being can have many, many evil spirits which will cause him to have many different personality traits that are not of their own being. And lastly, I would like to note that even thousands of years ago, it was of the culture to be dignified and push away that which scared people. These people were imploring the savior of the world to leave their town due to fear, and remaining dignified. There is truly no time to be politically correct when dealing with demons. This portion of scripture is telling us that when many demons are in one man, that in turn, the man will have many different behaviors that are in direct connection to the demon. Later I will point out specific demons and their specific behaviors, however, I would like to point out a few right now.

This man had no home. He lived in the mountains and the tombs, presumable out of the way of the main culture and people of the town. Day and night he cried and cut himself. Do you know any cutters? This is what people think of as a rather new method that is being used to cope with the stresses of life, however, I think it is clear here which demon is associated with people cutting themselves, and possibly forms of depression. Also the fact that he was able to break his chains because he had some type of superhuman strength should be noted here. Believe it or not, I personally have seen each of these traits among human beings in our day and age. I will not brush this off as some sort of coincidence, rather I will assert myself to help others rid their bodies of these demons that come from long ago; just as Jesus did.

Moving on, demons have emotions. This again, shows that they have personalities, confirming that we must see them as beings, even when they are not visible to most. There is a portion of scripture where James discusses the topic of faith and works. But it is interesting that in this passage, he refers to demons as having a physical emotion. James 2:19 (NKJV) ***You believe that there is one God. You do well. Even the demons believe—and tremble!***

We as humans tremble when we are scared, anxious, excited, or mournful. Yet here he says that demons believe, and tremble. This is an important thing to note when studying demons and their personalities. They are also knowledgeable. We have discussed how it is sometimes accurate when a psychic uses other supernatural powers such as demons to tell someone information regarding themselves. This is confirmed in numerous places in the Bible as well. In Acts 19:13-16 (NKJV):

> ***Then some of the itinerant Jewish exorcists took it upon themselves to call the name of the Lord Jesus over those who had evil spirits, saying, "We exorcise you by the Jesus whom Paul preaches." Also there were seven sons of Sceva, a Jewish chief priest, who did so. And the evil spirit answered and said, "Jesus I know, and Paul I know; but who are you?" Then the man in whom the evil spirit was leaped on them, overpowered them, and prevailed against them, so that they fled out of that house naked and wounded.***

This passage makes me laugh. I can just imagine a group of men trying to cast out demons with the name of

Christ but no belief in Him. However, on a more serious note, it makes me sad to think that there are actually people thinking that they are doing the work of Christ, fooling congregations and people, as well as themselves. I remember when I was full on using my third eye and giving people words that were coming from my "spirit guide/demon guides." I once pulled over in a parking lot to give a homeless man a word that I thought would help him with his addiction. I may have prayed for him afterward too, as I used to incorporate all of my spiritual knowledge. When I got home that night, I suffered from something very strange for the next two days. There is only one way that I can describe what happened to me in words. It is called withdrawal. I spent the next 48 hours shaking,, and had severe mood swings with excessive pain.. My explanation is that this man's demons jumped right onto me and began working in my life. They were able to do this because of my own sin and idolatry. We must be very careful how we are helping people, if not using the ways and beliefs of Jesus. Trust me when I say that inviting demons into your own life when trying to help others, definitely defeats the purpose in the overall picture. For it is written in Matthew 7:21-23 (ESV):

> ***"Not everyone who says to me, 'Lord, Lord,' will enter the kingdom of heaven, but the one who does the will of my Father who is in heaven. On that day many will say to me, 'Lord, Lord, did we not prophesy in your name, and cast out demons in your name, and do many mighty works in your name?' And then will I declare to them, 'I never knew you; depart from me, you workers of lawlessness.'***

Let us always strive to know Jesus first, and to seek first His kingdom and His face, so that these things cannot happen to us.

Continuing on, you see that this evil spirit knew of Jesus and even Paul but didn't know the Jewish priests. We must not underestimate the intelligence of demons. They know the Word of God because satan is their Lord, and satan of course knows the Word of God. The same way that God has a plan for your life and that of the lives of those you love, is the same way satan has a plan for your life and the lives of those you love. He will use people that are in the occult such as psychics, shamans, sorcerers, and witches to speak the destined path satan has for your life. It is when you seek this type of supernatural outside of the Holy Spirit that you willingly come into agreement with anything that is said. If you ponder, believe, or worry about the message received, then you have just come into agreement with a demonic prophetic type of word. This is why when people say they went to see a medium to talk to a loved one, or they went to a psychic as a joke, unfortunately the joke is on them. I will be the first to admit that this was me, and if this is you, Jesus will forgive you. He will remove all of the demons that you acquired through this type of abomination and breaking of the first commandment of having other gods. I know this first hand. Not only is it possible, but amazing how God can set us free and clean us up. However, I will warn the rest of you that if you want to explore any of this, know that the price that you will pay is insurmountable. It is so big that it could mean your life being taken, or quite possibly where you will spend eternity. Revelation 22:14-15 (NKJV):

Blessed are those who do His commandments,

that they may have the right to the tree of life, and may enter through the gates into the city. But outside are dogs and sorcerers and sexually immoral and murderers and idolaters, and whoever loves and practices a lie.

Demons also have knowledge about themselves. The demons inside of the demoniac said they were many inside of him. Demons have their own doctrines and lies. 1 Timothy 4:1-5 (NKJV):

The Great Apostasy

Now the Spirit expressly says that in latter times some will depart from the faith, giving heed to deceiving spirits and doctrines of demons, speaking lies in hypocrisy, having their own conscience seared with a hot iron, forbidding to marry, and commanding to abstain from foods which God created to be received with thanksgiving by those who believe and know the truth. For every creature of God is good, and nothing is to be refused if it is received with thanksgiving; for it is sanctified by the word of God and prayer.

This scripture, in particular, is important for end time conversation. We must stay very alert to what demons teach. Understand that they are working powerfully in people everywhere; in most churches and in every denomination, all new age situations and teachings, any and all cults, and of course in every occult activity. This is important for those that don't yet know

Jesus, but are searching, to read your Bible and find wise council from people that follow Christ.. This is of equal importance to those of you that know Christ. Do not underestimate the power that the devil will use in the end. He will pull the elect into an undercurrent of lies and hypocrisy, attempting to sear our conscience with a proverbial hot iron, forbidding us of Holy living.

Let's talk now about how demons use our bodies, minds, and souls. I left out our spirits deliberately, for if you are born again, born of water and of Spirit, then it cannot occupy your spirit. If you are not born again, I would urge you to read the story of Nicodemus so that it can testify truth to you, and I pray that God will remove all blinders, so that you too, can be saved. One of the biggest ways that demons use us is through deceiving us into believing other teachings. Anything that takes the focus from Jesus is basically how they deter us from true doctrine, or sets of beliefs. I was fast asleep one evening when I was awakened to big, beautiful gold floating letters. I looked upon these letters with awe and soon realized it was the very first chapter in the very first book of the bible. It said " in the beginning God created the heaven and the earth." It continued on until verse three or four, and then I began to see tiny purple letters forming in between each line of the beautifully written, gold lettering. Right between verse one and two was a language I could not read. I asked God what it was and He said it was the "Book of Lucy." I had no idea what this meant until He then said that Lucifer too wrote a book to be followed. He too wrote a book that is alive. When Jesus gave me the vision of the luciferian book that was shown in the same realm as the book of Genesis, He was showing me that lucifer had already fallen. His doctrine was already set to go out into the world deceiving people. There are some mysteries when trying to navigate through timelines, but when your given a revelation it is most assuredly for a purpose. Again, this is not to pump up or elevate satan in any way, rather, it is to become knowledgeable of our adversary, his beginnings, his present influences, and his ultimate demise.

Demons seduce people by erroneous doctrine, enticing them to do what is wrong, and act against the very words God spoke. Besides the obvious, why would this strategy work so well? One word. Enslavement! This is the master plan. If we can become slaves of the wrong master, it allows him to do what he wants with us, keeping us; continually oppressed and in darkness with no light nearby. And why do you suppose that is such a powerful plan? Because then we are puppets compelled by only the pull of satan himself giving all permission to torment us. And why do you think being puppets pulled on a string, tormented day and night is a brilliant plan? Because this leads us into complete defilement leading us down the "oh so wide path" to Hell. I want to break down each of these points to magnify the activities of demons and how they can harm us. Beginning with enslavement, Scripture teaches on such a thing. Galatians 5:1 (NKJV) ***Stand fast therefore in the liberty by which Christ has made us free, and do not be entangled again with a yoke of bondage.***

> ***For as in the day of Midian's defeat, you have shattered the yoke that burdens them, the bar across their shoulders, the rod of their oppressor.*** Isaiah 9:4 (NIV).

There is a positive side also to servanthood to Jesus

Christ in scripture, but we are focusing now on the opposite, that of satan. There is a compelling, destructive bond that he likes to get us locked in; through that of our sins, a generational problem, or wounds that have been collecting in our souls since childhood. For satan to enslave us, it gives him all of the power. This power leads into the capability of torment. We will discuss shortly how demons choose to torment us and with what emotions they pull on, however, I want to first refer to a scripture or two on torment. ***For God has not given us a spirit of fear, but of power and of love and of a sound mind.*** 2 Timothy 1:7 (NKJV).

In other words, if we don't have strength, love, or peace, then we have fear. Fear is an evil spirit that is obviously not from God. The following scripture stresses this point.

> ***There is no fear in love; but perfect love casts out fear, because fear involves torment. But he who fears has not been made perfect in love.***
> 1 John 4:18 (NKJV).

Tormenting spirits lead to a myriad of ***emotions*** that are used to keep us ***enslaved*** to satan. Compelling spirits, simply put, will give us an unnatural, overly compulsive want of something. Note the specifics further in this chapter as I zoom in on each spirit specifically.

Without getting into too many specific names, actions, and duties of each demon, I do want to point out a few of the higher ranked demons in the Bible. Although I have devoted much of my time to the study of demonology for this book, I feel that it isn't necessary for us to know all of them specifically. Jesus didn't feel the need to point out too many specific names in the Word of God, therefore, I will follow suit and only touch upon the ones that are most common, most active, and most detrimental.

A long time ago, God showed me that the more demons names and duties that you know, the more it seems they are being used instead of defeated. What I mean by this is that most people that study demons to the furthest degree are usually duped somewhere in the middle and get caught in the trap of the enemy. It is a dangerous road to travel my friends. If you have the desire to use demons in any way other than to step on their heads and make them your footstool, you will be greatly disappointed. You will find a deep level of darkness instead. Having said that, I would like to take a look at the leading problems that we face with demons, and teach you how to triumph over them. This triumph will only come from the name of Jesus Christ, and having the knowledge to use it.

Even in the writings of the Torah, false gods were worshiped which caused enmity with the true God of Israel. One of the most ancient and commonly known gods that the Caananites worshiped was that of the local land. His name is Baal, and this means "master," or "lord." This excerpt was taken from an article I read titled: *Baal, Ashtoreth and Molech - God's Old Testament rivals*[17]:

> An example of a local baal cult is called "Baal-peor" mentioned in Numbers 25:3, where the Israelites disgraced themselves in some sexual rites with the Moabites and worshiped the local god, incurring the wrath and punishment of their own god.
>
> Over the centuries, however, the cults of the

"Baalim" became merged and several specific larger cults developed. The best known of these was the cult of the Syrian god Melqart, worshiped by King Ahab of Israel and his "wicked" wife Jezebel. It was this Israelite worship of Baal which was challenged by the Hebrew prophet Elijah in his famous conflict with the prophets of Baal on Mount Carmel in I Kings 18, when he challenged the false prophets to bring down fire from heaven. When the prophets of Baal failed to do so, Elijah's God did so, resulting in the slaughter of the prophets of Baal by an angry mob. But the worship of the god was not so easily extinguished.

In the worshiping of Baal, it was the norm to be onlookers of sexual activities in a public type of setting. I can't help but think parallels watching films that fill our minds with unclean, dishonoring thoughts. This was a way to worship him then, so what do we call it now? In Isaiah 57:5-8 (NIV) it speaks of something that sounds like a Shakespearian version of our modern day strip clubs and booty calls.

> ***You burn with lust among the oaks and under every spreading tree; you sacrifice your children in the ravines and under the overhanging crags. The idols among the smooth stones of the ravines are your portion; indeed, they are your lot. Yes, to them you have poured out drink offerings and offered grain offerings. In view of all this, should I relent? You have made your bed on a high and lofty hill; there you went up to offer your sacrifices. Behind your doors and your doorposts***

> ***you have put your pagan symbols. Forsaking me, you uncovered your bed, you climbed into it and opened it wide; you made a pact with those whose beds you love, and you looked with lust on their naked bodies.***

Some may read this and think I'm being a bit "religious" or judgmental here, however, satan loves to deceive us. Do you think he is aware that we are an intelligent race? Yes, he is aware, and because of this, he must find ways to get us to be like those in ancient days, worshiping the pagan gods, although we are not aware that we are doing such a thing. It is not an overly religious thought that makes me aware of the music that is in circulation today. Because of my calling, I am often thrown into situations with darkness openly thrown in my face. I hear the music that is in the main stream. I also hear the demonic frequencies, or tones coming through the sound. As if the lyrics of degrading women, worshipping sex, money, and drugs aren't enough, women actually singing the degradation upon themselves as if it's somehow ok! When I look around and see naked women dancing on poles, with those poor souls worshipping Baal, while demonic energy is being poured into their drunken or drugged bodies, I have to say, I am not being scrupulous at all. I am observing with discernment what the Lord gave me. Oh, and we shouldn't think we "Christians" are mightier than thou. I see and use social media as a tool like the rest of the world, but. is it a Spirit of vanity or Jezebel in action?

Now we must ask God to gain understanding on how lucifer, the "ex-head of worship in heaven" is not only submerging the lost souls out there into defilement and blindness, but also the holy?! Why have we, as a generation, allowed satan to infiltrate every avenue that Jesus opened for us by His death? Why are we as women, sexually defiling ourselves and laughingly joining in, coming into agreement with demons? As we sing and dance to lyrics that degrade our entire gender? You think that you look sexy, but all you're doing is coming into agreement with the demon pushing this agenda, and showing men and the culture of this time, that it's ok with you to be put down, because you agree. This is nothing new that I'm speaking of, it has been around since the beginning of time. It may come in different forms, and in different packages, but it is the same demon. As stated above in Isaiah 57:8b (NIV), ***you made a pact with those whose beds we love, and you looked with lust on their naked bodies.***

Next I would like to discuss a fire god from ancient times named Molech[18].

> He does however have many forms of his name like that of Melech, Molech, Milcom, Melkom, Moloch, Molek, Malee,m Malik, Melek, Malkum, Melqart, Melkart, Milk, Melqarth, Kronos, Cronus, Malec or Malik. Molech represents the male principle of life and reproduction, while Ashtoreth represents the female principle of fertility. Assyrians and Babylonians called her Ishtar, while the Greeks and Romans called her Astarte, and North Africans call her Tanith. These two gods worked hand in hand in the Bible times. While anal sex between male and male worshipers and male and female worshipers was vowed as an offering to the goddess, the practice of burning of babies vowed an offering to Molech. He was an ancient fire deity; that of chemosh of Moab, and Melquart of Tyre.

Throughout the nation of Palestine his name was baal. He was also the deity of the Ammonites.

God warned the Israelites when they were entering the land that He had promised them. He warned them not to indulge in the practice of worshiping other gods. He spoke of many, and Molech was also mentioned here. In Deuteronomy 18:9-12 (KJV):

> ***When thou art come into the land which the Lord thy God giveth thee, thou shalt not learn to do after the abominations of those nations. There shall not be found among you any one that maketh his son or his daughter to pass through the fire, or that useth divination, or an observer of times, or an enchanter, or a witch. Or a charmer, or a consulter with familiar spirits, or a wizard, or a necromancer. For all that do these things are an abomination unto the Lord: and because of these abominations the Lord thy God doth drive them out from before thee.***

He speaks first of people making their children pass through fire, which is a reference to worshiping this god Molech. They would build great statues of Molech made out of bronze, with long arms and a hollow pot belly. He would have a head of a bull, and a fire would be built inside of him. This fire was used to worship him throughout the sacrifice of burning babies inside of the firey furnace, while the people played instruments loudly, deterring the family from hearing their children being burned alive. Nimrod, Baal, and Molech can be used somewhat interchangeably, making distinctions between the place, people, culture and time. The important part of understanding these false deities is not how popular they once were, rather how popular they are at the present. I realize that most people go through their lives unaware that satan has a master plan to torture us all for eternity. Let us be open to this matter so that we can allow God to speak profound revelations to us. I want to point out some things here to show that the worship of these demons has continued throughout time, with the children of God being deceived. Many others joined in knowingly, and unknowingly. In order for me to do this, I have to touch upon some elitist groups to make my point. Even though to we normal folk work day to day just to survive life and care for our families, the elitist groups behind the scenes are continuing the foundation of satan, that was laid thousands of years ago. Although that may not be some of our foundational premise, it still continues to affect us as it deters the lost from being found. If I haven't already showed the recklessness of worshipping these false gods, I would like to cite just a few more examples,

> ***And he defiled Topheth, which is in the valley of the children of Hinnom, that no man might make his son or his daughter to pass through the fire to Molech.***
> 2 Kings 23:10 (KJV).

> ***And thou shalt not let any of thy seed pass through the fire to Molech, neither shalt thou profane the name of thy God: I am the Lord.***
> Leviticus 18:21 (KJV).

> ***And Solomon did evil in the sight of the Lord,***

and went not fully after the Lord, as did David his father. Then did Solomon build an high place for Chemosh, the abomination of Moab, in the hill that is before Jerusalem, and for Molech, the abomination of the children of Ammon.
1 Kings 11:6-7 (KJV).

The reason I continue to make biblical references about this deity is because he is not only multifaceted, but has many derivatives of who he is, under the lordship of satan. Due to the almost unlimited information that can be found via the internet, or with a little investigation, I will not reference extensively on the elitist groups. The point I am attempting to make throughout this whole book is not whether satan and demons exist, rather that they are alive and well, penetrating the minds and bodies of our government leaders, military leaders, elitist groups that own the entire monetary systems of the global world, celebrities, our next door neighbors, and yes, us too! I first want to discuss quickly those of the Molech (also uses the symbol of an owl) and Baphomet worshipers who are among the elite people that meet at a place called Bohemian Grove. This relatively small group of people gather at least once a year to discuss government and global events. They are of the highest status and actually work to influence and determine factors of elections, military decisions, and with high profile., powerful celebrities. These celebrities worship satan's kingdom with orgies and occult practices. As I stated, there are plenty of references to learn about this, but I will cite some information about this meeting to further confirm what I am trying to establish in preparation of the end times. Here is an excerpt from an article on occult practices that takes place with global and international leaders[19]:

> Activist Alex Jones, infiltrated the Bohemian Grove, becoming the first journalist to capture and expose video of the bizarre, luciferian ceremonies that have been taking place there for over 120 Years. Alex Jones Has Blown Bohemian Grove Wide Open!" says John Sergeant of World of Wonder, UK Channel 4.
>
> During the ceremony globalist leaders from across North America and the rest of the world watch as a black garbed boatman delivers the effigy of a human being to be burned at the feet of the 40-50ft tall stone owl god by robe-clad druid-like priests.
>
> Participants openly worship the owl and scream for the burning death of the human effigy.
>
> Participants openly worshiped the owl. It appeared that low-level Acolytes were dressed in black and red robes, with higher-level priests in combinations of gold, silver and red. The high priest in silver and red robes repeatedly worshiped the owl, which he said was a symbol of Babylon and Tyre.
>
> The male-only elitist gathering chants and screams for the death of "Care" symbolized by a human body.

After many years of study on the matter of the Illuminati, and the freemasons, I have come to the conclusion that what they are doing, and how they are doing it, is somewhat irrelevant. What I mean is that these groups, and even individuals that worship satan are everywhere. They are scattered all over the earth. Some are the obvious worshipers like luciferian groups that we just discussed, and practitioners of the satanic bible, while some are less obvious like those who practice witchcraft, freemasonry, astronomy, study of zodiac, tarot cards, divination, necromancy, fornication, idolatry, and those seeking council from familiar spirits, spiritists and the dead. God often has me praying for celebrities. Normally He will place it upon my heart to pray for one or two for an extended period of time, and then He will use a divine appointment to allow me time to minister to them. This has happened on many different occasions. Even today I have a list of people that I pray for often, and am looking forward to the day God sets the appointment. They are usually very powerful meetings and His plan for them is obvious. Unfortunately, some of them return to complete disobedience and oppression shortly after. I feel that it is important to first depict the great deceptions satan is using behind the scenes and then focus in on how this effects the church and the unsaved. This will hopefully fully expose satan and his agenda, making it easier for us to prepare.

Next I would like to discuss Masons, also referred to as Freemasons. God showed me many years ago that this is the ancient organization from which the illuminati has been derived. Many people, Masons and those that are not, fail to escalate in the Kingdom of God due to this spirit of freemasonry that is either passed down from generations before us, or our own will to join. When this satanic organization has demons that pour through your bloodline from hundreds of years back, they become a strongman throughout your family line. God showed me this is a significant factor toward freeing many groups of cultures or religions. For the sake of not offending and initiating a debate between different religions, I will leave the actual names of these religions out of the book. I believe God will show you if and when it is necessary for you to understand this completely.

Freemasonry has, however, affected many humans with a root of magic in their bloodline. This demonic organization is said to have stemmed from the building of King Solomon's temple. God has shown me that the powerful demon behind this deceptive cult and organization is that of Baphomet. Speculative theories have arisen that the Knights Templar originated from Freemasonry. I am inclined to believe such speculations, as the Lord has shown me through prayer of a loved one. Detrimental deceptions that this demon has caused through such organizations throughout the history of time is overwhelming. It is nothing more that oppressive in nature. It is a secret tool that the devil uses to keep God's people blinded and immovable from such bondage. He is a strongman that has occupied many a man's house.

Because satan is a copycat, he used the same Hebrew numerology for Baphomet as he did when Christ gave the title as the cornerstone to Peter. This was symbolic of the building of the Temple and the mystic order that was being birthed through freemasonry, while also giving us a manuscript to study him and his agenda. A French man, by the name of Eliphas Levi, restored this worship of Baphomet in his early writings of *Transcendental Magic*[20]:

> Behind the veil of all the hieratic and mystical allegories of ancient doctrines, behind the darkness and strange ordeals of all initiations, under the seal of all sacred writings, in the ruins of Nineveh or

> Thebes, on the crumbling stones of old temples and on the blackened visage of the Assyrian or Egyptian sphinx, in the monstrous or marvelous paintings which interpret to the faithful of India the inspired pages of the Vedas, in the cryptic emblems of our old books on alchemy, in the ceremonies practiced at reception by all secret societies, there are found indications of a doctrine which is everywhere the same and everywhere carefully concealed.

Just to give a bit of reference here, I would like to cite an article with a section that describes Baphomet with accuracy: *The True Masonic Order*[21] by Henry Epps:

> The goat on the frontispiece carries the sign of the pentagram on the forehead, with one point at the top, a symbol of light, his two hands forming the sign of occultism, the one pointing up to the white moon of Chesed, the other pointing down to the black one of Geburah. This sign expresses the perfect harmony of mercy with justice. His one arm is female, the other male like the ones of the androgyne of Khunrath, the attributes of which we had to unite with those of our goat because he is one and the same symbol. The flame of intelligence shining between his horns is the magic light of the universal balance, the image of the soul elevated above matter, as the flame, whilst being tied to matter, shines above it. The beast's head expresses the horror of the sinner, whose materially acting, solely responsible part has to bear the punishment exclusively; because the soul is insensitive according to its nature and can only suffer when it materializes. The rod standing instead of genitals symbolizes eternal life, the body covered with scales the water,

> the semi-circle above it the atmosphere, the feathers following above the volatile. Humanity is represented by the two breasts and the androgyne arms of this sphinx of the occult sciences.

Later in this article it speaks of a modern day Baphomet statue being built in America. I want you to all be aware of the picture of Baphomet so as to connect today's uprising of this spirit with that of the same ancient spirit. Here are the details described in Wikipedia[22]:

> In 2014 The satanic Temple commissioned an 8 1/2 foot statue of Baphomet to stand alongside a monument of the Ten Commandments at Oklahoma State Capitol [66] "respect for diversity and religious minorities" were cited as reasons for erecting the monument.[67] After the Ten Commandments monument was vandalized plans to erect the Baphomet statue were put on hold as the satanic Temple did not want their statue to stand alone by the Oklahoma capitol.[68] The Oklahoma Supreme Court declared all religious displays illegal[69] and On 25 July 2015 the statue was erected near a warehouse in Detroit, as a symbol of the modern satanist movement.[70][71] The satanic Temple may take the statue to Arkansas where another 10 Commandments monument is proposed.[72]

In modern days, there have been many ceremonies that occurred on important days of satan worshipers' calendars. I want to take a look at just a few to prove that what we are dealing with is from ancient times, yet continues in our world, has our bloodlines in bondage, and keeps human kind blind even today. This article speaks about something that actually openly worshiped the demon of Baphomet with many prestigious people. From Vigilant Reports in *The Opening Ceremony of the World's Largest Tunnel Was a Bizarre Occult Ritual*[23]:

> Measuring over 57 km and costing over 11 billion Euros, the Gotthard Base Tunnel is world's longest and most expensive tunneling project in History. Going through the Swiss Alps, the tunnel took 17 years to complete and is said to be a symbol of European unification in a context of rising nationalism and closing borders.
>
> To celebrate the inauguration of this tunnel, an elaborate ceremony was presented in front of European dignitaries such as Chancellor Angela Merkel of Germany, President Francois Hollande of France and Italian Prime Minister Matteo Renzi. While most would expect an up-beat, celebratory ceremony, guests were rather treated to a disturbing show orchestrated by German director Volker Hesse, where a man dressed as a goat presided a strange ritual.

I would urge any of you to go and research this ceremony that took place in this celebration. It is extremely obvious and deliberate to whom they are giving homage, who it is working for, and who is involved. In giving one more example, I would just like to say that this is where our world is now, and we must not be ignorant of what the devil is pushing. We must no longer close our eyes to the abominations of God that are occurring on our earth. I am not sure that the opening of our eyes will stop it or delay it in any way, however, it will allow us to prepare for that which is to come; The great day of the Lord.

On the summer of 2016 there was an unveiling of the temple of Baal arch replica in Trafalgar Square in London[24]. They did however change the name from "the arch of the temple of Baal," to "the Palmyra arch of triumph." Regardless of what they are calling it or their attempts at covering it up, somehow with a veil, does not change the truth of it. Satan has an agenda to take over the world, and yes, that includes the USA. Will he hit opposition the whole way through? Absolutely, because the Bible says He will! This is great, but it does not mean that we idly sit by and watch God's precious creation of humans, being imprisoned slowly by the slimy carcasses of the skin of demons! Let's wake up and fight!

It was a beautiful summer day in Miami. The sun was bright and hot, the birds were chirping, and the sky was a beautiful clear blue. My day had started off pretty normal, until I received a message about a BBQ that a very well-known person was having. I prayed but didn't hear anything directly about whether to go or not to go. So I simply asked that God would order my steps. After some time passed, my friend was invited to the same BBQ and she was asking me to go with her. So I took this as a confirmation and headed out the door. It was a typical BBQ for a famous person on a famous island. It was the typical crowd, typical food, and typical vibe. Things didn't get supernatural until later.

My friend and I were sitting on the dock where the yacht and jet skies are parked. It was quiet. There were three or four other people on the dock. Everyone seemed to be enamored with whatever stories were on their snapchat. For a few moments, I was actually distracted by my phone as well, until I heard God's voice. I put my phone down, looked up into the sky, dark in the night, as each star twinkled with brilliance, and I said "Yes Father?" He very clearly spoke to me that I was to ask the man next to me if he was going to heaven or hell. Now understand that God has given me many words for people. Some have been tough to give, I will admit, but He had never before up to this point, asked me to approach someone with such a question.

I breathed deeply and thought about how one asks a random person such a deep question. He was browsing through his phone just relaxing, and God instructed me to ask such a thing! So I casually laid back looking up at the stars, turned my head to the right and said "So……… are you going to heaven or hell?"

He looked at me with such surprise, and not in a good way. He replied with "Hell of course."

This just opened up a thirty minute discussion about heaven, hell, Jesus, Christianity, and Islam. We talked and talked, and he argued and argued. He said that he trusted Muslims more than Christians. That comment alone was part of my prayer conversation for days. But, as the conversation continued, he was strong in what he felt, and he didn't think Jesus was God. I felt a bit defeated, but this wouldn't be the first time I had a saddening discussion with a stranger, and I was sure it wouldn't be my last. So we all stood up to go back into the house where everyone was getting ready for the next leg of the evening which would be some random club.

I heard the Lord say with fierceness, "Santaria, father's side, curse of death." It was so loud I almost asked if anyone else heard it. At any rate, while slowly walking on the deck to get to the house, I asked him if there was the practice of Santeria on his father's side.

He looked back at me and said "Why would you ask

me that?"

I said in return, "Because Jesus just told me that you have a curse on your life that came from the practice of Santeria on you father's side of the family." He was dumbfounded and wasn't sure what to do. I asked him if he wanted Jesus to remove this curse from him so that he could live a much different life. He joyfully responded with an excited "YES!" So I told my friend that I needed a moment to pray over him and took him aside next to the pool and began to pray. I asked if I could lay my hands on him and began to pray everything Jesus communicated to me. He received Jesus and the Holy Spirit into his life. I also prayed that the Holy Spirit would give him joy and show him that He is real.

The rest of the evening was supernatural for this man. God had begun His work in a man that no less than thirty minutes before, said that Jesus was only God to me because I was taught that. I feel like I am often telling people that Jesus is my God because Jesus showed himself to me.

I wasn't taught to walk in the supernatural by any pastor or any church. I wasn't taught to pray over those in need, and expect miracles by any preacher in a building. I do not have a problem with this happening of course. I believe many begin their journey with God in a church with a preacher, but I was taught to live the way Jesus wanted by Jesus alone. Pastors and churches are great! I love my pastor, my church, and all of my dear friends in the body of Christ, and they too, have taught me many things. But getting right down to the grit of my relationship with Christ, is Christ alone. Isn't it amazing that God will use us to help one person in a sea of millions? Isn't it amazing that because Jesus broke the curse over him, that he is free from a huge chain that was once tied to his life! This Leaves him in a place now to thrive as Jesus intended? This man keeps in touch regularly and he is now having experiences of his own. He had a word for a young woman he was randomly talking to. He has begun to search out God's word for life! His life will never be the same because God Almighty removed this demonic curse from his life. This is why I have so much passion concerning deliverance.

When God frees us from curses, and removes demons and strongholds from the root, it is life changing. It is so massive an event that anything you once thought to be true, will be completely repelled and the real truth will prevail. The truth of Jesus Christ of Nazareth is the most profound, life- saving revelation that any human could ever receive. With this, I will elaborate on the demons that cause specific symptoms in our lives. This list is not a definitive for every person or every situation. It reaches each person differently. There are many unique situations out there, however, this is to be used as a tool for a point of reference for you to pray about. Jesus will help you decipher what plan of action is necessary, and the list will help you narrow down possible explanations for your afflictions. The symptoms are not all listed in the Bible, but collected through personal experience, or other individual's personal circumstances.

In an attempt to make life a little simpler for everyone, I am going to break down the study of some spirits that plague our lives with an outline-type of format. Hopefully with this organization, you can pray, refer to the guide, and pray away these specific demons that affect your life. An outline is good, and having the names of specific demons will definitely help you, but remember that Jesus the deliverer is the only one that can communicate to you which spirit it is, what it has done to you, and how to get rid of it.

Deliverance can, more times than not, be a complicated process so that God can develop our senses and our supernatural ears to hear Him. I know in my life, He has used this method so many times. He will give me one word or one demon that I must then ask Him how to get rid of it. Also repentance and surrender are key to this process. Remember as you are going through this, that Jesus is doing it all for a purpose that is bigger than us. His kingdom is great and will reign inevitably, and I don't know about you, but I want to be a part of His plan and not my own; or more intently, I will not be a part of satan's kingdom or will. I will list some scripture to go with each of the spirits so that you can have references in the Word of God readily available to you when necessary. I want you to understand that when these symptoms arise, it is definitely a symptom of something much deeper. It is something manifesting out of the root of a strongman that lies much deeper in your soul. It is however, a good start when you have symptoms, as we can then begin to pray about the root.

Sometimes it's difficult to know when anything is wrong because nothing is rearing its head. Rest assured, within time, a symptom will occur, and you will need to get to the root. Like I warned, this is a process. This is especially true when dealing with fatal diseases and fatal problems. We will begin with this list as an introduction to pray and discover the root of the problem. God can do as He pleases whenever He pleases to do it. He may remove the root and all of the seeds and fruits with it. Or He may get rid of demons one at a time, down the long rope of them, leading to the root of the strong man of the situation. Perhaps removing them all at one time would be harmful to us, and because of His love for us,

He takes it at a pace our bodies and minds can handle. In my personal walk He has taken the smaller demons and symptoms over a period of time. I was surrendered and wanted them all gone, however. It has to be a desire for God to remove everything that is not of Him. We must pray about it with sincerity, and when it is perfect timing, God will remove it from us.

The following pages have charts for your reference so you can to identify any areas that need to be addressed. At the top of the chart you will see the demon or spirit that is affecting your life, while in the column it will describe the problems you may be suffering from due to the spirit's torment. As a disclaimer, these are not always the issue. God has so many mysteries and also created us so uniquely that He doesn't use a specific formula, but this is a tool to observe. Then entering into prayer, you can ask God if these are accurate to your situation. This is a simplified chart of spirits and symptoms/effects they can cause in our lives.

DEAF AND DUMB SPIRIT Possible Symptoms	**INFIRMITY SPIRIT Possible Symptoms**	**BONDAGE SPIRIT Possible Symptoms**
Blindness	Allergies	Addictions
Bruises	Arthritis	Ambition
Convulsions	Asthma	Anguish of Spirit
Crying	Bent body/spine	Avarice
Tearing	Blindness	Bitterness
Drives	Cancer	Living in sin
Drowning	Unknown Diseases	Broken Spirit
Ear problems	Frailty	Captivity of satan
Epilepsy	Fungus	Compulsion
Eye disease	Impotence	Coveting
Foaming at mouth	Lame	Poverty
Gnashing of teeth	Lingering Disorders	Servant of Corruption
Mental illness	Oppression	Shattered Life
Mute	Sinus Infections	Spiritual Blindness
Pining away	Virus Infections	Unforgiveness
Prostration	Weakness	
Schizophrenia	Unexpected Illness	
Self- mutilation		
Suicidal		
Wallowing		
Lunatic		
Seizures		
Burn		
Insanity		

Madness		
Tied tongue		
FEAR SPIRIT Possible Symptoms	**SEDUCING SPIRIT Possible Symptoms**	**ANTI-CHRIST SPIRIT Possible Symptoms**
Agitation	Allure	Against Christ and Teachings
Anxiety	Arouse	Attacks Testimony
Any excessive fear	Attraction	Deceiver
Apprehension	Deception	Denies Atonement
Carefulness	Enticement	Denies Deity of Christ
Doubt	Fascination with evil	Denies Power of the Word
Faithless	Hypocritical lies	Heresies
Fright	Seared conscience	Humanism
Heart Attack	Seducers	Lawlessness
Hermit	Sexual Desire Compulsion	Opposes Christ and Gifts
Horror	Temptation	Persecution
Inadequacy	Wander from truth	Suppresses Ministries
Intimidation	Apostasy	Teaches Heresies
Nervous Breakdowns	Win over	Vexes Soul
Nightmares		
Paranoia		
Rejection		
Stress		
Tension		
Terrors		
Timidity		

Torment		

ERROR SPIRIT Possible Symptoms	DEATH SPIRIT Possible Symptoms	DIVINATION SPIRIT Possible Symptoms
Argumentative	Abortion	Drugs
Contentious	Accidents	Enchanter
Defensive	Clumsiness	Fortune Teller
Doctrinal Error	Death	Intimidation
False Doctrine	Death wish	Horoscope
Form of godliness	Disease	Hypnotism
New age movement	Fear of death	Magic
Servant of Corruption	Fighting	Manipulation
Unsubmissive	Random acts of Violence	Rebellion
Unteachable	Suicidal	Soothsayer
New age beliefs		Sorcerer
Confusion		Stargazer
Indifference		Warlock
Homosexuality		Witch
		Zodiak
		Jezebel spirit
		Witchcraft spirit
		Familiar spirit

FAMILIAR SPIRIT Possible Symptoms	**JEALOUSY SPIRIT Possible Symptoms**	**LYING SPIRIT SPIRIT Possible Symptoms**
Astrologers	Anger-rage	Accusations
Clairvoyant	Apathy	Condemnation
Conjurer	Causes division	Deception
Consulter	Contention	Exaggeration
Drugs	Coveting	False burdens
False Prophecy	Cruelty	False prophecy
Medium	Emulation	False teachers
Mimicry	Envy	Flattery
Necromancer	Extreme competition	Gossip
Passive mind-dreamers	Hatred	Guilt
Peeping and Muttering	Indifference	Hypocrisy
Santeria	Murder	Lies
Spiritists	Retaliation	Religious bondages
Yoga	Retribution	Shame
Channeling	Revenge-spite	Slander
	Strife	Superstitions

PERVERSE SPIRIT Possible Symptoms	HAUGHTINESS SPIRIT Possible Symptoms	HEAVINESS SPIRIT Possible Symptoms
Abortion	Arrogance	Broken heart
Atheism	Boastfulness	Dejection
Child Abuse	Contentious	Depression
Chronic worrier	Domineering	Despair
Contentious	Idleness	Discouragement
Doctrinal error	Impatience	Excessive mourning
Evil actions	Intimidation	Hopelessness
Filthy mind	Manipulation	Insomnia
Foolishness	Obstinate	Loneliness
Fornication	Pride	Oppression
Homosexuality	Rebellion	Rejection
Incest	Rejection of God	Self-pity
Masturbation	Scornful	Suicidal thoughts
Pornography	Self-righteous	Suppressed emotions
Sex perversion	Smug	Torn spirit
Twisting the Word	Strife	

WHOREDOMS SPIRIT Possible Symptoms	**RELIGIOUS SPIRIT Possible Symptoms**	**WITCHCRAFT SPIRIT Possible Symptoms**
Adultery	Outward appearance obsession	Super spiritual
Overly ambitious	Condemnation	Rebellion
Chronic dissatisfaction	fear	Emotional manipulation
Fornication	Oppressive legalism	Intimidation
Gluttony	Self effort	Immorality
Greed	Religious tradition	Soul ties
Idolatry	Worldly tradition	Control
Love of money	Fear of change	Wickedness
Overeating	Manipulation	Mantras
Prostitution (body, mind, or soul)	Need to figure God out	New age beliefs
Unfaithfulness	Competitive in ministry	Confusion
Worldliness	Overreact to carnality in the church	Divination
	False holiness	Astronomy
	Salvation by works	Horoscopes
	Guilt	
	Unhealthy fear of God	

	Perfectionalism	
	Criticism	
	Division	
	Error	

LEVIATHAN SPIRIT Possible Symptoms	**JEZEBEL SPIRIT Possible Symptoms**
Discord among brethren	Accusation
False witness	Aggression
Fixating on problems	Anti-God
Twisted words	Attention seeking
Twisted hearing	Belittling
Unable to confront personal faults and dysfunctions	Heretical
Wicked plans in the heart	Indecision
	Intellectualism
	Promiscuity
	Sexual immorality
	Sexually abused
	Sexually abuses
	Witchcraft

If you look through this list and it is overwhelming you because of the similarities you see in yourself, don't panic! We have discussed the fact that we all fight demons whether we like it or not. We have also discussed the fact that demons are either in us or around us in an attempt to steal, kill, or destroy us. This is where we must sincerely take a look at our relationship with God. If you can relate to any of these symptoms, not only have I proved a very valid point, but I pray that I am also showing you that you need Jesus the deliverer.

When we look at our lives and sift through all of our sins, or all the bad we have done, honestly speaking, we will never be able to know them all. There are too many, for everyone in the world, Christian or not. Am I being assumptive? How do I know this? I know this because this is why God sent Jesus to die for us. He knew that we would always mess up. He knew that we would never be able to remain perfectly pure, without blemish. This is an important thing because unholy things cannot be in the presence of God. He sent Jesus to die and pay for each and every sin, each and every disgusting, wretched, and defiling thing we do, He paid for it. So let us honor the King of Kings, and in humility ask for His help. If you haven't yet given permission to take complete control over your life, then now would be the time. I have included a prayer at the end of the book to help guide you through this process.

8 SEEK HIS FACE

So the question is, do we go into super battle mode with spiritual warfare and attack every demon that is interfering in our lives, or is it time to seek God and pray? Having both of these practices is most necessary to a successful walk while we are here on earth. However, there is a time and a season to press in on different levels, with different intentions. The reason I felt this was important enough to put in this book is because God has shown me numerous tools in different seasons that I have endured, to not only achieve a level of success in my prayer life, but also to have a clear picture of walking with Jesus on this earth. It is most definitely our responsibility to seek God, to hear His words, and to obey Him. This is not always easy. In fact, more times than not, it is extremely difficult.

I like to think of when Paul and Silas were traveling from city to city preaching about Jesus everywhere they went. When they first traveled through the towns of Amphipolis and Apollonia, they came to Thessalonica. He taught the Holy Scriptures in the synagogues there and explained the death and resurrection of Christ. Some believed the truth he was sharing, while others were jealous. So they were accused of being guilty of treason against Caesar. They said this because they were professing allegiance to another king; King Jesus. After being released, they continued on to the city Berea. Here they spoke the truth of Christ in the synagogues again, with many of the people open and curious to God's word. Acts 17:11 (NLT) says ***They searched the Scriptures day after day to see if Paul and Silas were teaching the truth.*** Now as they were making headway in Berea, the very men that caused them trouble in Thessalonica came to stir up more trouble for them. My point in using this quick excerpt is to show you that life is a chain of events. Now, obviously the big picture of the world, God, humans, etc. is a whole different study, but still a chain of events that began with:

> ***In the beginning God created the heavens and the earth. The earth was formless and empty, and darkness covered the deep waters. And the Spirit of God was hovering over the surface of the waters.***
> Genesis 1:1-2 (NLT).

Paul and Silas were hitting opposition wherever they went, yet they stayed focused on the face of Jesus. It is important to seek Him, and His face and to continue to push through all opposition that you will meet. This is the picture I see; Paul and Silas face forward chasing Jesus' face, while behind them, were the Thessalonians chasing them. Behind the Thessalonians was a powerful force of evil chasing them; only causing them to pursue Paul and Silas. So as we run for Jesus and His Kingdom, we must be aware of that which is behind us. I always find it important to spew fire balls from my heels as I am running, with a full armor of God on, because I know what is behind me. However, it is of equal importance to keep my face forward as I run, looking only to seek His face. Jesus paid a price when He died for us, and we too will pay a price. It is an inevitable truth of the law of death and resurrection with Christ that will be either that which pushes us forward on with Him, or that which will stop us from living our full potential in Christ while here on earth. It will be your choice how far you are willing to suffer with Jesus. It will be your heart and your desire to say "yes" or "no" to the suffering that will be required of you. As God has slowly, graciously, and lovingly burned things out of me that did not belong, He too, has slowly and graciously shown me the principle I am talking about here. So just face forward with the full armor of God on, while spewing fire at the enemy behind you and you will most assuredly continue to climb this mountain of life. Earlier in chapter 3, I quoted scripture in Ephesians about spiritual warfare in part, and now I would like to finish the scripture as it pertains to this message.

Ephesians 6:10-18 (AMP) describes The Armor of God:

> ***10 In conclusion, be strong in the Lord [draw your strength from Him and be empowered through your union with Him] and in the power of His [boundless] might. 11 Put on the full armor of God [for His precepts are like the splendid armor of a heavily-armed soldier], so that you may be able to [successfully] stand up against all the schemes and the strategies and the deceits of the devil. 12 For our struggle is not against flesh and blood [contending only with physical opponents], but against the rulers, against the powers, against the world forces of this [present] darkness, against the spiritual forces of wickedness in the heavenly (supernatural)***

places. [13] Therefore, put on the complete armor of God, so that you will be able to [successfully] resist and stand your ground in the evil day [of danger], and having done everything [that the crisis demands], to stand firm [in your place, fully prepared, immovable, victorious]. [14] So stand firm and hold your ground, having tightened the wide band of truth (personal integrity, moral courage) around your waist and having put on the breastplate of righteousness (an upright heart), [15] and having strapped on your feet the gospel of peace in preparation [to face the enemy with firm-footed stability and the readiness produced by the good news]. [16] Above all, lift up the [protective] [c]shield of faith with which you can extinguish all the flaming arrows of the evil one. [17] And take the helmet of salvation, and the sword of the Spirit, which is the Word of God. [18] With all prayer and petition pray [with specific requests] at all times [on every occasion and in every season] in the Spirit, and with this in view, stay alert with all perseverance and petition [interceding in prayer] for all God's people.

So before we delve into this portion of the scripture, I want to point out some facts from history from the time of this writing. A common Roman Legionary from 60AD was heavily armed[25]. He carried a short, fat, stabbing sword called a gladius. This was used with a lethal effect in the close-quarters at which Romans fought. He wore this on his right side and could draw it with his right hand while steadying his shield with the other. On his left, he would wear a shorter dagger called a pugio[26]. This was used as a backup in case the sword failed him. He also carried a javelin in which the shorter one would throw around 30 meters and the heavier one around 15 meters. This was the weaponry carried as a part of life. Every legionary wore body armor as well, which consisted of overlapping, hinged plates of iron that were laced and buckled in both the back and front with leather straps. The iron helmet that was worn had a brow ridge that would deflect any downward blows. It also had cheek plates and a wide brim at the neck for further protection. They too, wore a large wooden, oblong shield with a metal boss in the middle. It would stop missiles, protect against sword slashes and act as a battering ram. According to Merriam-Webster, a battering ram is "a large and heavy piece of wood or other material that is used to hit and break through walls and doors."

Now that we have looked at an actual description of the armor from the time this scripture was written, and have a detailed picture in our heads, let's take a look at certain key words from the scripture. First, and most obvious is "armor." In the ***Strong's Concordance*** the Greek meaning of full armor is this:

> 3833 panoplía (from 3956 /pás, "every" and 3696 /hóplon, "weapon") – properly, a complete set of defensive and offensive armor (weapons), i.e. everything needed to wage successful warfare; (figuratively) the full resources the Lord gives to the believer so they can successfully wage spiritual warfare. In this way they do not fight for victory – but from His victory!

While another key word in this scripture in the Greek, according to ***Strong's Concordance*** is the word "evil" (Eph. 6:13):

> 4190 ponērós (an adjective which is also used substantively, derived from 4192 /pónos, "pain, laborious trouble") – properly, pain-ridden, emphasizing the inevitable agonies (misery) that always go with evil.

Now that we have clearly explained how we are armored and why we are to armor ourselves daily, I would like to quickly make clear why each part of the armor is necessary. The helmet of salvation is a protection for our souls to understand our salvation. If we put this helmet on daily, we will never lose sight or question our own salvation through the redemption of Christ. It will help to desist of all things and theologies that attempt to turn our minds from the true doctrine of Jesus Christ and His promise of salvation. The breastplate of righteousness is that of our purity and rightness of life. This piece of armor protects us from neck to belt on all sides of our bodies. Some say that this is the area in our body where our soul and spirit is carried. If this is true, it would make sense to put on a protective covering of righteousness over this portion of our bodies so that we can remain all day in the righteousness of Christ. Next is the belt of truth. Now I am aware that many people and many religions have a different idea of the word truth, however, there is only one truth that is true. Jesus said to the Jews that believed Him in John 8:31-32 (NIV) ***"If you hold to my teaching, you are really my disciples. Then you will know the truth, and the truth will set you free."***

It is this truth He is speaking of when we are to put on the belt of truth. It is the truth of Christ's teachings that we choose to believe, that sets us apart from others; hence setting us free because we know such truths. This is a centralized theory in which the belt goes around us protecting us from lies and deceit. This is a necessary truth. Next I will discuss the shoes of the good news. This one is mostly self- explanatory. But I am going to quote ***Strong's Concordance*** Greek: 2097 here because I like what it says.

euaggelizó: to announce good news
Original Word: εὐαγγελίζω
Part of Speech: Verb
Transliteration: euaggelizó
Phonetic Spelling: (yoo-ang-ghel-id'-zo)
Short Definition: I bring good news, preach good tidings

Definition: I bring good news, preach good tidings, with or without an object, expressing either the persons who receive the good news or the good news itself (the good news being sometimes expressed as a person).
euaggelion: good news
Original Word: εὐαγγέλιον, ου, τό
Part of Speech: Noun, Neuter
Transliteration: euaggelion
Phonetic Spelling: (yoo-ang-ghel'-ee-on)

Short Definition: the good news, the gospel
Definition: the good news of the coming of the Messiah, the gospel; the gen. after it expresses

sometimes the giver (God), sometimes the subject (the Messiah, etc.), sometimes the human transmitter (an apostle).

I love the last part where the translation is "human transmitter." That is us. We walk through earth wearing our shoes of the good news as armor, to transmit the gospel of Jesus Christ to the world.

Next on the list is the sword of the spirit. This is loaded with complexities and is necessary for us to have understanding of this piece of armor. From Strong's number 3162, sword, in Greek means:

> Mechaira: a large knife, used for killing animals and cutting up flesh. A small sword, as distinguished from a large sword. Curved sword, for a cutting stroke. A straight sword for thrusting.

And Spirit, in the Greek, according to Strong's number 4151:

> pneuma: wind, spirit
> Original Word: πνεῦμα, ατος, τό
> Part of Speech: Noun, Neuter
> Transliteration: pneuma
> Phonetic Spelling: (pnyoo'-mah)
> Short Definition: wind, breath, spirit
> Definition: wind, brcath, spirit.
> HELPS Word-studies
>
> 4151 pneúma – properly, spirit (Spirit), wind, or breath. The most frequent meaning (translation) of 4151 (pneúma) in the NT is "spirit" ("Spirit"). Only the context however determines which sense(s) is

meant.

[Any of the above renderings (spirit-Spirit, wind, breath) of 4151 (pneúma) is always theoretically possible (spirit, Spirit, wind, breath). But when the attributive adjective ("holy") is used, it always refers to the Holy Spirit. "Spirit" ("spirit") is by far the most common translation (application) of 4151 (pneúma).

The Hebrew counterpart (rûach) has the same range of meaning as 4151 (pneúma), i.e. it likewise can refer to spirit/Spirit, wind, or breath.]

So as I read this, the very breath of God used in the armor in accordance with that of the sword, becomes a very powerful weapon. I immediately think here of the verse in Hebrews 4:12 (AMP):

> ***For the word of God is living and active and full of power [making it operative, energizing, and effective]. It is sharper than any two-edged sword, penetrating as far as the division of the soul and spirit [the completeness of a person], and of both joints and marrow [the deepest parts of our nature], exposing and judging the very thoughts and intentions of the heart.***

Wow! The Word of God is God alive and active, so this means when we speak the Word of God, it acts as a knife, sharper than any two-edged sword, going to the deepest part of any situation. This is why when Jesus was tempted by satan in the dessert where God sent Him, He only quoted scripture. If we are carrying the sword of the spirit, or the Word of God with us all day every day, it will be that word spoken that saves our lives. While this concept and truth is very powerful and I would love to go into further detail of how this sword of the spirit can also divide soul and spirit, I will acknowledge that a deliverance minister may use this in a most effective way. We will now move to the last bit of armor mentioned, and discuss the shield of faith! Oh what a beautiful shield! Oh what a glorious bit of safety the Lord gives us to use daily! The Shield of faith that protects us from the fiery arrows of the evil one! Our fidelity and faithfulness to Christ that His Spirit gives us in measurement of His faith, is that which will protect us from the arrows that the devil shoots at us all day long. He is clever, so they come in many forms, whether it be a flat tire, a fight with your spouse, traffic congestion, or even thoughts that aren't your own, your shield of faith allows them to bounce off. If your shield needs to grow in size, it is wise to pray that Jesus would give you more of a measure of His faith to survive. And that which we ask, according to His will, will be given to us. Perhaps once you have learned or been reminded of putting these biblical principles into action, you too will laugh in the face of the devil; and also look forward to the next adventure that God has for you! It is written in Acts 17:27 (NASB) ***that they would seek God, if perhaps they might grope for Him and find Him, though He is not far from each one of us.***

The part of this particular scripture that is intriguing to me, is that we seek Him though he is not far. If the living spirit of God lives in us, then why must we seek Him? Isn't that like looking for a pair of glasses that are already sitting on your head, or seeking for your cell phone that you're currently talking on? In Strong's Hebrew: 1245. בָּקַשׁ (baqash),[27] The first few words are most descriptive, giving us a better picture of this word "seek.:" aim, beg, begging, concerned, consulted, demand, desire, eager, hold, inquire, investigate, plead, pursuit, request, require.

I assure you that soe of you reading this are seasoned Christians that already understand this concept, and there may be others who are asking what my point is. My prayer is that this message will become universally dispersed throughout the nations to seek God! For me, personally, I didn't understand this until Jesus came to me with an assignment . . . At some point, years back, I was curious and hungry for the passion of God. I would wake up and wonder what exactly God would do with my life if I let him. He will not infringe on our will He gives us a choice to follow him, or to stay blinded. He gives us opportunities for our hearts to be softened, for our eyes to be opened, and for our spirits to be merged with His. I'm reminded of Pharaoh in the book of Exodus with the great prophet Moses. Hopefully most, if not all reading this, know the story of Moses and the exodus of the Israelite people. But Pharaoh was given opportunity after opportunity to turn to the God of Israel and set the people free, yet his heart was hard and he could not see what disaster was coming. Each and every plague set him to a new level of anger and frustration, but the last, where he would lose his one and only son, I can imagine was the most detrimental of all.

God gives us moments in time to turn to him. He gives us supernatural appointments with angels, children of God, mercy, grace, and miracles from heaven to turn our hearts. It is a choice; it is up to us whether or not we willingly respond to these moments in our lives or not. Can you think of a time like this in your life? A time when God was calling you and you answered, or chose to ignore Him? I have many of both that I can reflect on. Some bring sorrow to my heart that I was so stubborn, and others bring joy that He loves me so much He continued to pursue me until I heard His voice.

When Jesus came to me in an open vision, I will now do my best to describe one of the most meaningful and beneficial moments of my life. It just so happened that I was on fire for the Lord. I was two years in deep study of demonology and theology. I had ignored God's call for my life for three years straight, but finally when I heard, I obeyed. I remember I was having dreams of babies at this time. Each night I would have different dreams of little babies all night long. To me, it was exciting! I wanted more children and just knew that God was confirming that I will in fact have more. I was also praying each night that God would translate me to Heaven and speak to me for just a moment. I know it was a lot to ask considering I had ignored Him for most of my life, but I felt He had forgiven me and would love to hang out with me in heaven.

It just so happened that around this same time, that my church had invited two guest speakers to come and minister to us: Adam Thompson, and Adrian Beale. As I got dressed and put together what I needed, I asked God if He would take me to Heaven while at the meeting, or at least have a word for me so I could better do His will. I arrived and as the meeting began with beautiful worship and prayer, I realized there were angels in the room. I saw one large angel standing over one of the men. I thought it was a great start to a meeting! As they began to call people up to minister, I felt my spirit explode inside! The Holy Spirit was stirring inside of me like I had never experienced. When they got to me, they prophesied that I would have a deliverance ministry, helping those who are in bondage to break free. I had heard this before, and it made sense because God had already established gifts of discernment and the study of demons in my life. But then I fell to the floor with the power of God over me. The man continued to bless others with a word from the living God Jehovah, when suddenly he turned back to me, pointed at me lying on the floor while I was slain in the spirit and said, "You will go to the third heaven and you will write books. You have books inside of you." I immediately cried! I was ecstatic that God had heard my prayers about going to Heaven to hang out with Him. The books were a nice message but I didn't take it all too seriously. I decided to hold that one in my heart until God wanted to bring it forth. I figured maybe I would write a book when my life was more put together and I had accumulated more wisdom. But in this meeting, the man also told me he saw a double portion of the Elijah spirit falling upon me. Again, it was a wonderful thought, but I didn't quite understand the meaning of it.

A few days passed, and I was so excited about my dreams, my calling, and just being with God, that I was praying and seeking His face for hours each day. I had been doing this for over a year at this point, but it was overwhelmingly powerful after this meeting. The presence of God had never felt stronger in my life. It was around 8:00 in the evening. Somehow I was home alone, which was a rare happening in itself. But I was in my room praying when right before my eyes a man in a glowing white robe showed up. He sat in a chair in front of me, and his face was so bright that I could not look directly at him. I knew that I knew that I knew it was my father, Yeshua. He pointed His finger at me and as I tried not to be distracted by the detailed white robe, the shining face, or the fact that I was sitting across from the "Savior of the World," He said, "You will write a book, and the title will be 'Spiritual Survival Kit for the End Times'!" I said in return, "Father, I will! But I don't know how to write a book, or what to write about." He then gave me a list of many different subjects and specific studies to begin my book writing process. And as suddenly as He showed up, He disappeared. He was gone, but He left me with an assignment and some information to begin. I immediately wrote down all I remember Him saying to me, and the title of the book. Did I mention this all happened when I was seeking God?

Part of truly seeking God is to seek all facets of God. The senior pastor at my church spoke on how our relationships with our spouses are similar to our relationships with God. Similarly, when we get married, we take on all that belongs to our spouse. We have to take on their good and their bad, their baggage and their backpacks. This is essentially what Christ does for us. In return we too must die with Him, and take up a cross. To try and look at every aspect of God would be truly unfathomable, as I believe it would just be too overwhelming, so if we break down and discuss a few branches that stem from His tree, it will allow us to focus in and magnify certain aspects of His great love. My attempt is to give a few hands-on, specific tools we have that can make the process of seeking Gods face, His Kingdom, and His son, a bit more elementary. It is not God that is complicated, but it is the understanding and the revelation or lack thereof that can make it tricky.

First I want to talk about wisdom and revelation. Wisdom was with God from the beginning. She was there when He created the heavens and the earth. So to seek her would be pleasing to the Spirit of God. This is the very same Spirit that hovered over the waters when the earth was without form and void. Seeking wisdom would be a two-fold benefit. Not only would we benefit from having wisdom and pursuing it daily, but we would be blessed to honor God with obedience to His instruction. As Paul wrote in Ephesians 1:17 (AMP):

> ***[I always pray] that the God of our Lord Jesus Christ, the Father of glory, may grant you a spirit of wisdom and of revelation [that gives you a deep and personal and intimate insight] into the true knowledge of Him [for we know the Father through the Son].***

Wisdom and revelation are Spirits that dwell with God's great abundance. It would bless us to seek them. I love the poetic way that King Solomon wrote about wisdom in the book of Proverbs. Although it is a bit lengthy, the intrinsic and ethereal concept that he grasps when speaking of wisdom, makes it personal, yet informative so that it is attainable, allowing it to actually penetrate our understanding. Words without wisdom do not hold much value, while words that are revelatory from our Creator hold wisdom. Let's take a look at how King Solomon, the man known to be the wisest in the Bible, depicts wisdom his in Proverbs 8 (AMP):

The Commendation of Wisdom

1 Does not wisdom call,
And understanding lift up her voice?

2 On the top of the heights beside the way,

Where the paths meet, wisdom takes her stand;

3 *Beside the gates, at the entrance to the city,*
At the entrance of the doors, she cries out:

4 *"To you, O men, I call,*
And my voice is directed to the sons of men.

5 *"O you naive or inexperienced [who are easily misled], understand prudence and seek astute common sense;*
And, O you [closed-minded, self-confident] fools, understand wisdom [seek the insight and self-discipline that leads to godly living].

6 *"Listen, for I will speak excellent and noble things;*
And the opening of my lips will reveal right things.

7 *"For my mouth will utter truth,*
And wickedness is repulsive and loathsome to my lips.

8 *"All the words of my mouth are in righteousness (upright, in right standing with God);*
There is nothing contrary to truth or perverted (crooked) in them.

9 *"They are all straightforward to him who understands [with an open and willing mind],*

And right to those who find knowledge and live by it.

10 *"Take my instruction rather than [seeking] silver,*
And take knowledge rather than choicest gold,

11 *"For wisdom is better than rubies;*
And all desirable things cannot compare with her.

12 *"I, [godly] wisdom, reside with prudence [good judgment, moral courage and astute common sense],*
And I find knowledge and discretion.

13 *"The [reverent] fear and worshipful awe of the Lord includes the hatred of evil;*
Pride and arrogance and the evil way,
And the perverted mouth, I hate.

14 *"Counsel is mine and sound wisdom;*
I am understanding, power and strength are mine.

15 *"By me kings reign*
And rulers decide and decree justice.

16 *"By me princes rule, and nobles,*
All who judge and govern rightly.

17 *"I love those who love me;*

And those who seek me early and diligently will find me.

18 *"Riches and honor are with me,*
Enduring wealth and righteousness (right standing with God).

19 *"My fruit is better than gold, even pure gold,*
And my yield is better than choicest silver.

20 *"I, [Wisdom, continuously] walk in the way of righteousness,*
In the midst of the paths of justice,

21 *That I may cause those who love me to inherit wealth and true riches,*
And that I may fill their treasuries.

22 *"The Lord created and possessed me at the beginning of His way,*
Before His works of old [were accomplished].

23 *"From everlasting I was established and ordained,*
From the beginning, before the earth existed, [I, godly wisdom, existed].

24 *"When there were no ocean depths I was born,*
When there were no fountains and springs overflowing with water.

25 *"Before the mountains were settled,*

Before the hills, I was born;

[26] *While He had not yet made the earth and the fields,*
Or the first of the dust of the earth.
[27] *"When He established the heavens, I [Wisdom] was there;*
When He drew a circle upon the face of the deep,

[28] *When He made firm the skies above,*
When the fountains and springs of the deep became fixed and strong,

[29] *When He set for the sea its boundary*
So that the waters would not transgress [the boundaries set by] His command,
When He marked out the foundations of the earth—

[30] *Then I was beside Him, as a master craftsman;*
And I was daily His delight;
Rejoicing before Him always,

[31] *Rejoicing in the world, His inhabited earth,*
And having my delight in the sons of men.

[32] *"Now therefore, O sons, listen to me,*
For blessed [happy, prosperous, to be admired] are they who keep my ways.

33 "Heed (pay attention to) instruction and be wise,
And do not ignore or neglect it.

34 "Blessed [happy, prosperous, to be admired] is the man who listens to me,
Watching daily at my gates,
Waiting at my doorposts.

35 "For whoever finds me (Wisdom) finds life
And obtains favor and grace from the Lord.

36 "But he who fails to find me or sins against me injures himself; All those who hate me love and court death."

This portion of scripture is packed full of wisdom, new ideas, old ideas, and a perception we should all take note of. Wisdom stands at the top of high places meaning she has the view from which she has all advantages. She can see what no one else is capable of seeing, to better benefit one's life. She only speaks truth. She knows not lies and abominations, but only the moral compass God had for us from the beginning of time. The things wisdom says to a person that has understanding are plain and comprehensible, whereas to a man without wisdom, he cannot comprehend. He says that wisdom is better than rubies and that no desires that we hold can compare to it. I think this scripture makes it more than clear that wisdom has been around from everlasting. She has been with God from the time we know of His appearance, and this is a treasure for all to know. I tell you this because God has shown me that asking for wisdom truly is a gem to receive according to James 1:5 (NLT) ***If you need wisdom, ask our generous God, and he will give it to you. He will not rebuke you for asking.***

As God was talking to me about how important having wisdom is, He showed me this scripture. My goodness, how simple was it to attain wisdom. Why had I not thought to ask for this before? It was because I wasn't aware that wisdom was a literal part of God. I wasn't aware that wisdom was with God from the beginning of the formation of earth and humanity. So when God began to show me this view point, things became clearer from the get-go. Why is this important for the advance into the end times? Wisdom, understanding, knowledge, and discernment, all go together for the war that we will soon face. Without wisdom, we lack a certain secret understanding that God is more than willing to give us if we ask for it. It is as if you have the perspective of a botanist when studying flowers, or the expertise of a neurologist when studying the brain. It is an inside blueprint of whatever we need, when we need it. Wisdom from God, is as if He handed you the answer key of a multiple choice test. Is this not important? Let's look at Proverbs 4:6-10 (NKJV):

> ***6 Do not forsake her, and she will preserve you; Love her, and she will keep you.***
> ***7 Wisdom is the principal thing; Therefore get wisdom. And in all your getting, get***
> ***understanding. 8 Exalt her, and she will promote you; She will bring you honor, when you***
> ***embrace her. 9 She will place on your head an ornament of grace; A crown of glory she will***
> ***deliver to you." 10 Hear, my son, and receive my***

sayings, And the years of your life will be many.

This is not only about being promoted and bringing in honor to yourself, but rather, honor to God whose grace will crown your head; His grace will cover that which you need, simply by receiving wisdom. I don't know about you, but if His grace covers a multitude of sins, then wouldn't it be appropriate to seek His face, and seek what wisdom, and allow His grace as an ornament to be placed on our heads?

I was praying about what He wanted me to write about in this chapter, when I heard Him clearly say James 1:5. So the hunt began. I searched all scripture that I could find associated with wisdom. At this time I was well aware that I lack all kinds of wisdom, but that God is more than willing to help me attain some. I began to pray for it. I asked every day, and every night if He would give me more of His wisdom according to the scripture James 1:5. Within the next two weeks of doing this, I received so much information that I had trouble retaining it all. There were things happening in my dreams, in my mind, and in visions. I wasn't exactly specific about what topic in my life I was asking to receive wisdom on, however. I was actually quite vague. I did this purposely as I desired to know what God considered wisdom. I wanted to know what God wanted me to gain knowledge about. To me, this was much more important than gaining any knowledge about something in my personal life that wasn't God's first priority. This is not to say that asking God for wisdom on specific things in our lives isn't appropriate; it most assuredly is. As a matter of fact, I would suggest you do that too. However, in this case, for me, I was seeking to know His heart, His wisdom, and His concerns, not my own.

The more we seek His desires, and the more we seek all that He is, the more we will grow in the wisdom He offers us. This isn't for the weak, or for the selfish; this is something that one usually doesn't ask for if not nudged by God. Most people are so caught up in their own personal gains, issues, or thoughts, that they can't even focus enough on God to ask what is on His heart. Pray for this yearning. Pray for this love to grow inside of you because it is He that will fill you with the wisdom that counts. The wisdom that we need for the end times is much different from the wisdom that helps us along in everyday life. In this time that is nearing, most of what we know will fall by the wayside due to such a severe change in circumstances. Also transitioning from freedom in a free world to survival in a not-so-free world will catch many unprepared. We are so used to freedom that once it is gone, and we have no phones or computers, televisions or cars, most people will enter into panic instead of wisdom. We can talk about our children for an example. Do they even have the slightest clue what it means to not be able to go to the grocery store and grab some bread or milk? Do they have the slightest clue of what life relying on only God looks like? I am not saying that it isn't a blessing from God that you have enough money on a regular basis to buy the necessary things you need for your family. That is, of course, a blessing from God. It makes me think of Matthew 6:25 (NKJV):

> ***"Therefore I say to you, do not worry about your life, what you will eat or what you will drink; nor about your body, what you will put on. Is not life more than food and the body more than***

clothing?"

This scripture along with many others, tells us that our Father will take care of us. Hence the blessing of being able to feed your family is, of course, not a coincidence, rather it is a blessing from God. The importance of not worrying about it is also a little nugget of wisdom to hold onto. But again, being prepared for what the Bible says about the end times is also wise. Should we be worried about it? Not if you are sincerely walking with Christ. If you are, then you will not be deceived in the end. If you are not deceived in the end, then you will not partake of the mark of the Beast, but rather, you will be marked by God for protection! But without wisdom to know what is to come, and without preparation, I think difficulties could be multiplied. Let us take heed of all scripture, for if we ignore it in part, then we will be deceived in part. In Matthew 22:29 (NIV) ***Jesus replied, "You are in error because you do not know the Scriptures or the power of God."***

Yes, I may have taken this verse out of context, but this verse alone says it all, no matter the context it is within. We are simply in error to not know the scriptures. It is the scriptures that Jesus spoke back to satan when He was sent to be tempted. It is here, within these writings that Jesus refers to Exodus 3:6 and 3:15. God Himself is referring to His own word! So let us be wise and take note of all that it says. So as parents, is it not our duty to protect and teach them? Is God not protecting and teaching us?

We have to start to look at this time on earth as very short, yet also very temporary. We have to begin to look at the times in which we live as utmost importance to live out that which God has encoded into our DNA. I must say, it was not of my own brilliance that this urgency of surviving the end times was birthed. It was only Jesus that has put this fire deep down in my spirit. All I did was begin to pray with no agenda. All I did was seek Him, and His desires, and this is where it led me. We do not, obviously, all have the same calling and assignment while we are here, so I imagine yours will differ from mine. However, we must be diligent in walking this destined life out completely, taking care, not to only fulfill bits and pieces. We must also be diligent not to allow the enemy to steer us in the wrong direction leading us to our ultimate demise.

That is why God has me writing this book and discussing these issues now, as He is allowing us time to prepare for what is to come. God loves all of us so much, and with His brilliance and persistent love, He will guide us to not only survival, but triumph. As most of us know, the King of Kings, the Lion of the Tribe of Judah, is triumphant already, but He will take His reign in the end; and when every knee shall bow to Him, it will be too late to ask for wisdom or to prepare for anything, including the end times. It will then be that time in which God desires us to prepare for now. In Numbers 27:12-23 informs us that Joshua had been chosen to succeed Moses, but that should also remind us of Deuteronomy 3:22 (KJV) ***Ye shall not fear them: for the Lord your God he shall fight for you.***

Wherever it is that God places us in life, however great or small the task seems, we shall fear not, because it is our God that fights for us. I would like to end this chapter with a simple prayer. I would like you to speak it aloud and with sincerity:

Father God, the Father of Abraham, Isaac, and Jacob, as I sincerely seek your face, I ask that you would instill in me, wisdom and truths that would surpass all that you have shown me thus far in my life. Please forgive me for my lack of knowledge of your precious scripture, and for not being diligent in seeking your Kingdom first. Let today mark the first day that the molecular structure of my DNA, in which you have encoded with your predestined plan for my life, become unified with your Spirit, allowing me to be transformed into the human being you planned for me to be. Let no man, no evil, no enemy, no person, no animal, and no agenda stop this from coming to pass! In the name of Jesus Christ of Nazareth I declare this decree over my life, and it shall be established! Amen

9 THE HOPE IN DELIVERANCE

What do people think of when they hear the word deliverance? Perhaps they think of the Exodus movement, when God delivered a people into the Promised Land and out of slavery and bondage. Or maybe they think of a package that needs to be delivered from the Post Office tomorrow. Or maybe they think of the movie the exorcist. I think each person has a different view of this word, and there is good reason for it. I don't think it has many definitions, rather, it is viewed differently by individuals. This is because it is up to God, and if you know God, then you know He rarely uses any kind of worldly formula when doing anything. In some religions, and in some parts of the world, people use the word exorcism, thinking that this is how to define deliverance. My opinion definitely differs from this idea. Let us begin with a definition of the word deliverance, according to Merriam-Webster:

> noun de·liv·er·ance \di-ˈli-v(ə-)rən(t)s, dē-\
> Simple Definition of deliverance: the state of being saved from something dangerous or unpleasant

God once said to me that He would take that which is in me that doesn't belong, and fill the left over space with Himself. I assure you that I had no idea what He meant. Please don't misunderstand, I thought I understood, but boy was I wrong! As life continued, and He began removing things from me, it was confirmed that I had no clue what He was talking about. I remember the first time I heard the words "deliverance prayer." I wasn't quite sure what it meant, but it was a biblical terminology so I was okay with whatever it meant. I began to look up scripture and testimonies of this thing called deliverance. These are some of the scriptures I used to gain understanding on this matter from the KJV.

> ***The righteous cry, and the LORD heareth, and delivereth them out of all their troubles.*** Psalms 34:17.

> ***Then they cried unto the LORD in their trouble, and he delivered them out of their distresses.***
> Psalms 107:6.

> ***And he said, The LORD is my rock, and my fortress, and my deliverer;***
> 2 Samuel 22:2.

> ***And call upon me in the day of trouble: I will deliver thee, and thou shalt glorify me.*** Psalms 50:15.

> ***Confess your faults one to another, and pray one for another, that ye may be healed. The effectual fervent prayer of a righteous man availeth much.***
> James 5:16.

I sought the LORD, and he heard me, and delivered me from all my fears.
Psalms 34:4.

Stand fast therefore in the liberty wherewith Christ hath made us free, and be not entangled again with the yoke of bondage. Galatians 5:1.

But the LORD said unto me, Say not, I am a child: for thou shalt go to all that I shall send thee, and whatsoever I command thee thou shalt speak. Be not afraid of their faces: for I am with thee to deliver thee, saith the LORD. Jeremiah 1:7-8.

And ye shall know the truth, and the truth shall make you free.
John 8:32.

The Lord knoweth how to deliver the godly out of temptations, and to reserve the unjust unto the day of judgment to be punished:
2 Peter 2:9.

[14] *For sin shall not have dominion over you: for ye are not under the law, but under grace.*
[15] *What then? shall we sin, because we are not under the law, but under grace? God forbid.*

[16] *Know ye not, that to whom ye yield yourselves servants to obey, his servants ye are to whom ye*

obey; whether of sin unto death, or of obedience unto righteousness?

17 *But God be thanked, that ye were the servants of sin, but ye have obeyed from the heart that form of doctrine which was delivered you.*

18 *Being then made free from sin, ye became the servants of righteousness.*

19 *I speak after the manner of men because of the infirmity of your flesh: for as ye have yielded your members servants to uncleanness and to iniquity unto iniquity; even so now yield your members servants to righteousness unto holiness.*
Romans 6:14-19.

If ye abide in me, and my words abide in you, ye shall ask what ye will, and it shall be done unto you.
John 15:7.

I beseech you therefore, brethren, by the mercies of God, that ye present your bodies a living sacrifice, holy, acceptable unto God, which is your reasonable service. And be not conformed to this world: but be ye transformed by the renewing of your mind, that ye may prove what is that good, and acceptable, and perfect, will of God.
Romans 12:1-2.

And when he had called unto him his twelve disciples, he gave them power against unclean spirits, to cast them out, and to heal all manner of sickness and all manner of disease.
Matthew 10:1.

It appears in these scriptures that God is doing something powerful. It also seems that when He refers to deliverance, that someone is receiving something, whereas when He refers to casting out, that someone is doing something. As I have already shared with you, God has assigned me, if you will, with the gift of discernment and He also uses me to command demons out of people and places. Although we are all capable of doing this, I want to talk about what this means to me.

Many Christians already know the meaning and have been delivered from something evil before. Unfortunately, many Christians have not been through deliverance, either because they don't understand it, they don't want it, or they don't believe they need it.

I have noticed that for the most part, deliverance is put aside, ignored completely, or it is done in some back room with an appointed elect few that manage the situation. It is obvious to me, however, that deliverance is not always a pretty thing. It is also not always an easy thing and can sometimes be a time-consuming process. It most assuredly is not always a composed or polite thing. The very root of deliverance goes against that which we're taught from an early age. Sit up straight! Cross your legs! Shhhh, you're being too loud! That wasn't a monster under your bed, it was your imagination! But if there is anything that I will share in this chapter that holds the utmost importance, it is this; there is HOPE in deliverance. After salvation and being baptized in the Holy Spirit, and having the infilling of the Holy Spirit, deliverance from demons, curses over an individual, or generational curses in the blood line of a family, must be dealt with! The exhilaration and freedom that Christ gives us in the midst of deliverance is just one more opportunity to get much closer to God. It is just one more opportunity by the grace of God to reach new levels of intimacy with Him. Just when you think you've got God all figured out, He will change it up for your astonishment.

There is a place that we will all reach one day. I don't know the timing, as it is different for everyone, but it is inevitable. In this place, there is a sense of being alone; yet you are not. In this place, you are vulnerable, but only to Him. In the deepest, most pure moments of honesty when you will allow yourself to feel the presence of the Father, is when He will change you. It is when He will take your mountain and command it to move for you. It is when you know He is present, not by a tingle, or even because the word says so, but because you have just figured out that He truly has your back. He shows in a very tangible way that HE IS GOD! Unlike any human, unlike any animal, unlike any friend, unlike anything here on earth, The Almighty Father, has your back. He may let you fall, but if He does, know that there is a purpose behind it, and that it is His love. You may be asking yourself how that is possible. I realize it may sound a bit contradictory saying that God will let us fall, but it's because He loves us. From my own personal experience I can tell you that it is when He allowed me to fall the hardest that I learned the greatest lessons. They were also the times when I realized why God allowed it, and how I saw His love and faithfulness more than ever. He will lift you up, if in all sincerity you want him to.

Most likely, we don't even understand this moment until it is upon us.

Let me explain this with a moment in my life when God decided to remove the addiction of smoking cigarettes from me. I had smoked for almost two decades at this point in my life. I was hiding it from my church folk, in fear that I would be judged. Those who love me voiced their concerns, regularly annoying me about this nasty habit. I had tried to quit smoking many times before, but only had success one time, and that lasted a mere six months. When stress would hit, I couldn't take it anymore and went to every length to get a cigarette. Addictions are powerful. They not only chemically change our bodies and brain functions, but a demon has latched on deeply to our soul creating a need to fill. This is why addictions are always so very hard for people to conquer. Some say they don't have enough "self-will," while others blame it on their upbringing or sad, sorry lives. Understand that none of these are correct. It is a demon. It can be a very strong demon with a very deep root. Have you ever seen anyone that does drugs and can stop whenever they want? Have you ever seen a drinker or smoker that can stop cold turkey at the drop of a dime? This isn't the way satan chooses to work in that person's life. The person never opened a door that attracted the demon of addiction. For me, smoking was a very deep-rooted addiction. I, of course, never knew this. I thought I was just like my family and this is the way it was. I thought this for so many years. It wasn't until after deliverance of other demons that God began talking to me about the problem. Did He take it right away? No. First I had to ask God what the problem was. I had to reach out to God and knock on His door and ask Him why I couldn't quit this atrocious habit. I also had to ask why I liked it so much if it was bad for me and my body.

God began to speak about my childhood. In a vision He took me back to the tender age of 14 when I stood at a bonfire party in the woods. I was young and impressionable and thrown into the party scene because of my siblings' influence. My parents that loved me and cared for me were unaware that I was at a party in the middle of the night. Now this is a time in a child's life when demons are circling to destroy, like that of a shark as he circles his prey. I had already decided not to drink, or do drugs because I saw my siblings doing it and I did not like how they acted. So that night, oh so long ago, satan convinced me that smoking a cigarette was my best bet of looking cool, to fit in without anything altering my mind or the way I acted. Years passed and I continued to smoke. Even when I met Jesus three years after this, I continued to smoke. I walked with the Lord for years, still smoking. I did not realize that it was a seed that the devil planted. I did not realize that it had developed into a demon. But at this moment, twenty years later, He showed me with an unmistakable power that this was a powerful demon rooted into my soul. Before the actual day of deliverance, I prayed for about two months that God would show me why I smoke, and how to break it off of my life. He showed me self-esteem issues that were formed that night at the party. He showed me a comfort of the cigarette that developed as I smoked when stress hit. Yet I prayed to be healed from all of this. Nothing happened!

Later when I went out of town to visit some family, while driving by myself, I heard God say "I am going to take smoking from you soon." I was ecstatic! I could not have been more excited. As my family continued to bother me about my smoking problem, I assured them that Jesus told me He was going to "take it from me." About two weeks later, it is an understatement to say that He took it from me. God himself came, and ripped it from my soul. This strong demon attached itself to my soul, and Jesus pried him piece by piece from me. This may sound very dramatic as I am explaining it, but it was very dramatic. Jesus allowed satan to attack me that day. As I was working on some notes for a study I was preparing, I began to get very dizzy. The room began to spin, but I recognized it. It was a demon that moves closely with the spirit of anxiety. So I immediately took authority and command it to leave.

The heaviness of this spirit lifted a bit, but not enough. I went to a more private place, as I was in public when it hit, and I commanded the demon to loosen its hold on me. I repented and commanded. Nothing changed. I was trying to walk to my car, but the dizziness was so severe, I was running into the walls. I was scared, but when I got to my car, the dizziness lightened up a bit and I drove less than a mile to my home. I texted my brother and friend from church to pray for me as I knew something was wrong. I put the phone in my purse and proceeded to my front door. I entered, and suddenly the entire room spun with abandonment. I could see nothing! I could do nothing but cry in fear. I prayed with so much sincerity asking God to forgive me for whatever I had done to allow this attack on my life. I verbally and openly broke all agreement with anything that was allowing this demonic action to take place. I had never in all my years of loving Jesus prayed with such surrender and sincerity. I attempted to kneel and pray, but the dizziness overcame me and I became very nauseous. I had to vomit from the incessant spinning. I wobbled to the bathroom at this point, and when I threw up, I expected the coffee I had ingested that day to come out, but this is not what happened at all. When I opened my mouth to vomit, pure white foam began to pour from my mouth. I didn't understand what was going on. I wasn't aware that I was receiving deliverance. I thought that I was under a physical attack from satan, which I was, but that is all I thought.

Although this was a physical attack on my life, going to the hospital didn't cross my mind. I knew this was satan upon me in a very powerful way. I knew God saw everything that was happening but wasn't doing anything to stop it. As I lay on my bed, so dizzy I couldn't breathe, God showed me an angel. He was in the corner of my room just standing there. As I lay in a fetal position, like a baby in a mother's womb, I could barely breathe. With slow, shallow breaths, I breathed like a fish out of water. Short, shallow breaths were all that my body would allow. I could only stare at the angel because whenever I looked anywhere else, the room continued to spin. I thought I was dying. I thought that satan had won this battle because of my own sin. This scripture about death went through my mind a few times. ***For the wages of sin is death; but the gift of God is eternal life through Jesus Christ our Lord.*** Romans 6:23 (KJV).

I had run out of all options except to sit and stare at an angel and trust Jesus with my life. About four hours into this tormenting time of my life, my phone rang. It was my brother returning my phone call. I answered the phone and uttered a few soft words that I could get out, explaining what was happening. He began to pray. He prayed and we came into agreement on this thing to loosen its hold. He had a few words of knowledge about what was going on, spoke the authority of Christ, and just like that, I could see again. The room was no longer spinning. I was no longer nauseous. I felt like me again. I learned this day that when you're in trouble with satan and you have done all that you know how to do, come in agreement with a brother or sister in Christ, and watch it leave. Now I was very happy indeed that this torment lifted! I was very happy indeed that I learned a few lessons through the experience. I was a bit upset with God though. Did I have a right to be? Nope, we never have a right, but our flesh just jumps right in and takes entitlement. I couldn't wrap my mind around why He would allow such a horrific moment to occur. Why would my Father in heaven, that loves me so endearingly, allow the devil himself to wamp me?

I was having trouble praying, as I feared another incodent and I cried for about three days straight. But the morning after this great event, I realized I did not want to smoke. I realized I had no craving for a cigarette. After all this time, had he taken it? Well, I still to this day have not smoked a cigarette. When people ask, I simply tell them that Jesus ripped the smoking right from me, and that is exactly what He had done. This demon was so adhered to my soul that he had become a part of me. Jesus had to allow satan to intimidate me into a place of complete surrender in order for me to give God one-hundred percent permission to take it from me. All the times that I had prayed in the past about it was a good start, and a good try. However, that thing's hold was so strong it was an actual root in my soul. God had to rip him off of me. Slowly, piece by piece, Jesus Christ of Nazareth delivered me from a dangerous entity. The Gospel is translated to "the good news" for reasons that may be unseen to you. He is so, so good. But, I tell you this, if you do not yet know Jesus as your Savior, and you know you long to find a sense of wholeness and long for more in your life, take up your cross with Him, and watch each and every void be filled.

When dealing with deliverance, it is important to remember that you are becoming involved with two invisible spiritual kingdoms. The kingdom of satan and the Kingdom of God are at war and because you are in the kingdom of God, this makes you automatically involved in war with the kingdom of satan. It is also important to understand that you are not dealing with people, rather you're dealing with the wicked spirit of infirmity that could have latched on to a soul after having a back surgery. You you are dealing with the Jezebel spirit that crept in after an uncle molested his nephew. I feel it necessary to press the issue of knowing that if you could see into the spirit realm, which some of you can, then you would also see it as a priority to point out that a demon is there. Once this perception is understood from your spirit man, you will begin to see the capabilities that Jesus has. You too, will begin to see how deep His love is for a person when He rips a demon from him. It has got to be one of the most amazing things I have ever experienced!

I will admit, however, that satan and his demons do not like this ministry at all. I believe, like Derek Prince,(my favorite deliverance minister,) that the deliverance ministry exposes not only his kingdom, but the reality that he even has one. The devil has been doing a great job in the western world, protecting his exposure. Pastors typically aren't dealing with demons, but instead dish out "feel-good" sermons that help people stay in the dark. Let me make clear here that I do not think it is all pastors, all churches or all ministries that avoid dealing with demons and deliverance. I know there are some that are following the guidance of the Holy Spirit. I am speaking of some, and those that I am speaking of may not even know that they are keeping this God given gift from the body of Christ. There are also the churches that hide deliverance. I have a problem with this because Jesus never hid casting out demons. As a matter of fact, in the majority of Jesus' ministry written about in the scriptures, He cast demons out and healed the sick almost everywhere He went. He did this out in the open, after teaching a lesson, or when He traveled by foot from city to city. He would be stopped or compelled to help someone. Sometimes it was used as a teaching tool, but always as an act of love for his brothers and sisters.

So I ask you, why is it that the majority of churches leave this very obvious biblical teaching, out of their services? My best guess is fear; fear of what others will think. A fear of the typical behavior of a manifestation, fear of what the demon will cause the person to do, and fear of the demons themselves. I hope that by this point, we all know that fear is a demon in and of itself. I think it is time to get deliverance out there in our churches, but also wherever else the Holy Spirit may send the minister. Most people within satan's kingdom are not even aware they are in it because they are in the darkness. They cannot see! We must use discernment when dealing with conventionalism, traditionalism, and all religion, or we too will begin to be blinded by satan's kingdom.

One of the greatest problems with people today is their lack of knowledge concerning removing demons. I find it a regrettable fact, and a disservice to Jesus to ignore the portion of scriptures where Jesus cast out demons. I hear so many differing opinions about the ministry of deliverance. Opinions are great, but it is imperative that we do as Jesus did, in all aspects of His life. God has brought it to my attention that one of the biggest hindrances from churches and individuals offering deliverance from demons is due to a lack of understanding and embodiment of our authority. Our very identities in Christ as royalty and sons of God give us an automatic right to remove demons. This change in our DNA that occurs when we are born again, holds the same Spirit of Jesus. Although we are not gods, we must do as Jesus instructed and walk as He walked. We must assert our authority and participate in the Kingdom of Heaven on earth. He purposely equips us to war for God's Kingdom while here. This is done by using all of the gifts that He has given to us. The scriptures clearly state what Jesus has called His disciples to do:

> ***And he called the twelve together and gave them power and authority over all demons and to cure diseases,.***
> Luke 9:1 (ESV).

> ***"And these signs will follow those who believe: In My name they will cast out demons; they will speak with new tongues; they will take up serpents; and if they drink anything deadly, it will by no means hurt them; they will lay hands on the sick, and they will recover."***
> Mark 16:17-18 (NKJV).

Jesus gave us power and authority to move in the supernatural world, bringing the Kingdom on earth, by curing diseases and binding demons. This is not only a biblical command, but also an assumed position of leadership in a Kingdom. A beautiful picture of this authority that He gives to us is found in 2 Kings 2:7-9 (NIV):

> *7 Fifty men from the company of the prophets went and stood at a distance, facing the place where Elijah and Elisha had stopped at the Jordan. 8 Elijah took his cloak, rolled it up and struck the water with it. The water divided to the right and to the left, and the two of them crossed over on dry ground. 9 When they had crossed, Elijah said to Elisha, "Tell me, what can I do for you before I am taken from you?" "Let me inherit a double portion of your spirit," Elisha replied.*

I just love how Elijah moves in the Spirit of God! But take a look at what God had given him in order to move in this way. The gift he held was so profound, that his predecessor Elisha, wanted not only to have his exact gift after he went, but a double portion of it. Whenever I read this, I first thank God for all He has blessed me with, and then I am reminded that we have been given a great mantle from Jesus himself. We have been commanded to walk as He walked. We have been commanded to cast demons out of people! To remove legions of unclean spirits from people. To tell the man on the street corner in the wheelchair to get up and walk! To speak to the cancer and command it to die at the root. This responsibility is great indeed, but He has given us all the keys to His kingdom. Are you bold enough to take them, thank Him and begin to walk in power?

It was a colder, windy day when I was driving down the highway and God showed me a gold crown upon my head. It was glorious in size, and brilliant in color. I couldn't take a breath until the vision had ended. I began to ask Him many questions about this crown. What did it mean? Could it be as obvious as the fact that I am royalty in His kingdom, or was there more to it? I began to study and pray, day and night until one day Jesus began to download information and scripture to me about the authority I hold. But it wasn't just about holding this authority, it was also about my actions being directly related to how I use it and the power behind it.

When God speaks to me about the importance of deliverance, He tells me of the grievances in his heart concerning the churches' outlook. I know that I have already touched upon this in an earlier chapter, however, as I'm writing, He is instructing me to give this even greater emphasis. It is the church that is detracting from the important of deliverance. Not to say they don't believe in it, or that it is not of God; (most true believers do believe in it and say that they abide in the teachings of it) but I see more and more people saying things like, "We need to focus on Jesus and not the devil." I, one hundred percent agree that we need to focus on Jesus, however, devils, unclean spirits, and satan are mentioned throughout scripture. Even though God has all authority over them, and we already know that the victory has been won through Christ, it does not mean that we do not have a job to do down here. Otherwise, why would God have given us authority over these things? Wouldn't it be pointless to have authority and be a king and a priest in a Holy Kingdom if there was no reason for authority?

I agree that the emphasis in our lives should be that of Jesus, His word, His power, His promises, His goodness, His love and His Holiness, but He has made it clear to me that lessons must be learned about satan and his demons. I know that if some of us would have been using the secrets of spiritual warfare in our lives, we would have less struggles and oppositions in life, but especially in the end times. It will be imperative to utilize our power in Christ to survive. Everyone in the body is capable of this because we are the children of God. There are also many functions to each part of the body of Christ. In each of these parts, we will function at our highest capabilities when needed. As I have said, this is why God has been preparing each person in their own callings. Because mine is deliverance, He has not only given me an urgency to point out the power that is attained in Christ through deliverance, but also to warn people now to prepare. I hope that it is understood that it is part of our responsibility as a Christian to do all the things Christ did, and more!

First I would like to offer a scripture that asserts our authority and does it with clear motivation. Luke 10:18-20 (NLT):

> ***18 "Yes," he told them, "I saw satan fall from heaven like lightning! 19 Look, I have given you authority over all the power of the enemy, and you can walk among snakes and scorpions and crush them. Nothing will injure you. 20 But don't rejoice because evil spirits obey you; rejoice because your names are registered in heaven."***

It is crystal clear that He is giving us authority over all the power of the enemy. There is a reason He has done this. While the Lord handles things on His own, without even a mention of the devil, He says we can walk among snakes and scorpions and crush them. Call me crazy, but walking and crushing are two action verbs. Action meaning, we actually have to do something. Also, if praying prayers, speaking the promises of God in the scripture, and declaring decrees can change outcomes and cause miracles to manifest, then it would be no different from commanding demons like Jesus did. It would be no different than using our authority to cancel any agenda satan is planning to use against us. When God allowed satan to use his power over certain prophets in the Bible, it was always His decision that mattered. In our lives it is the same. There were times, too, when a prophet took it upon himself, using his authority through prayer and fasting, or speaking to a demon, that God was pleased with him for doing so. He taught them lessons about rebuking demons from people. Matthew 17:20-21 (NKJV) states:

> [20] ***So Jesus said to them, "Because of your unbelief; for assuredly, I say to you, if you have faith as a mustard seed, you will say to this mountain, 'Move from here to there,' and it will move; and nothing will be impossible for you.*** [21]
> ***However, this kind does not go out except by prayer and fasting."***

In this text, Jesus explains the importance of faith and how it can not only benefit our personal lives, but also the lives of others. He also explains that sometimes we will not be able to cast a demon out unless we take certain steps, like fasting and praying. These lessons are invaluable! They are the very essence of deliverance itself! But even more importantly, He says to rejoice about our names being in heaven. So let us always rejoice in our salvation and His love for us.

Mostly those who use His authority, speak His name, and walk in the Holy Spirit will not be harmed by anything when casting out demons. Remember the three Jewish exorcists in Acts 19:11-20 (NKJV):

Miracles Glorify Christ

> 11 *Now God worked unusual miracles by the*
> *hands of Paul,* 12 *so that even handkerchiefs or*
> *aprons were brought from his body to the sick,*
> *and the diseases left them and the evil spirits*
> *went out of them.* 13 *Then some of the itinerant*
> *Jewish exorcists took it upon themselves to call*
> *the name of the Lord Jesus over those who had*
> *evil spirits, saying, "We exorcise you by the Jesus*
> *whom Paul preaches."* 14 *Also there were seven*
> *sons of Sceva, a Jewish chief priest, who did so.*
> 15 *And the evil spirit answered and said, "Jesus I*
> *know, and Paul I know; but who are you?"* 16
> *Then the man in whom the evil spirit was*
> *leaped on them, overpowered them, and*
> *prevailed against them, so that they fled out of*
> *that house naked and wounded.* 17 *This became*
> *known both to all Jews and Greeks dwelling in*
> *Ephesus; and fear fell on them all, and the name*
> *of the Lord Jesus was magnified.* 18 *And many*
> *who had believed came confessing and telling*
> *their deeds.* 19 *Also, many of those who had*
> *practiced magic brought their books together*
> *and burned them in the sight of all. And they*
> *counted up the value of them, and it totaled fifty*
> *thousand pieces of silver.* 20 *So the word of the*
> *Lord grew mightily and prevailed.*

Without a personal relationship with Christ, deliverance and casting out demons can be a dangerous thing. And don't bother trying to con God either, He knows whether or not you truly have a relationship with Him. I would suggest not using His name when removing demons if you are into other occult practices as well. These men were in family lines of high priests, yet they were afflicted. Don't just bypass the part of the text that says they "***leaped on them, overpowered them, and prevailed against them.***" These holy men ended up running out of a house naked and wounded. Why would they be naked? Perhaps the demons caused complete mental breakdowns, or gave them pain all over their bodies. We can speculate here why they were naked and physically, mentally, emotionally and spiritually wounded, but I definitely think it is more important to understand how God's authority works. Demons do not have power over Jesus or His followers, but they are not to be underestimated.

It is important to understand that when we pray, there is conflict. If you don't think that satan is constantly trying to hinder your prayers from being answered, you are most assuredly wrong. We know his mission and goal, so I will not reiterate these points on just how he does this. The greater the prayer, mission, or purpose of something, the greater the opposition from satan. If we are constantly praying for our own personal gain, we may or may not see less opposition from satan. But, if our prayer or mission is to further the Kingdom of God or His glory, the opposition can and most likely will become great.

Remember when Daniel was praying for the nation of Persia and it took 21 days for the angel to come say that his prayers have been heard? It didn't take twenty one days to be heard, it took twenty one days for the angel to say to Daniel that he heard them. You see, because of the courtroom system of heaven, there are many legalities that come into play when requesting something of great significance. No matter what we think, God is a judge that will make mandates on our life, according to legal rights and interactions in our lives. If satan has a legal right to stop something from happening or a prayer from being answered, then that is it. We must assert our authority and also put into practice the lessons Jesus teaches us in the Bible in order to break all legal rights given to satan. Some of these rights are given to him through our bloodline, so you may think that you are innocent. This is not the case. A curse or legal right given to satan through a bloodline must be renounced and repented for. Yes we have to repent for our ancestors. I was once asked during a deliverance why we had to do this, but as soon as I explained and they repented, it was lifted and the demons associated, fled. These are some of the problems that I see when demons will not leave a person. Satan has a legal right to perform negatively in their lives. So what is it that we are supposed to do? When Jesus compares heaven to a courtroom setting, He speaks about prayer. Prayer and persistence is the key to breaking legal rights that satan holds over you. Luke 18:1-8 (NKJV) gives us a parable to gain some understanding on the matter:

The Parable of the Persistent Widow

[1] Then He spoke a parable to them, that men
always ought to pray and not lose heart, [2]
saying: "There was in a certain city a judge who
did not fear God nor regard man. [3] Now there

was a widow in that city; and she came to him,
saying, ‘Get justice for me from my adversary.’ 4
And he would not for a while; but afterward he
said within himself, ‘Though I do not fear God
nor regard man, 5 *yet because this widow*
troubles me I will avenge her, lest by her
continual coming she weary me.’” 6 *Then the*
Lord said, “Hear what the unjust judge said. 7
And shall God not avenge His own elect who
cry out day and night to Him, though He bears
long with them? 8 *I tell you that He will avenge*
them speedily. Nevertheless, when the Son of
Man comes, will He really find faith on the
earth?”

There is something about persistently petitioning God on matters we know are His will for our lives, yet we have not yet seen manifested on earth. Just as this unjust judge gave in to the widow due to her persistent questioning, will not our Father in heaven be so great as to give us innocence in our court case with satan? He will. An excerpt from an article by Robert Henderson[28] is very helpful when describing this idea of a judicial system. He says:

> Revelation chapter 12, verse 10 tells us that there is an accuser of the brothers that is accusing us before God day and night. This word "accuser" is the Greek word kategoros and it means a complainant at law, against one in the assembly. This is the same word used to describe the woman's "adversary" in Luke 18. Satan's strategy to keep us from what God has for us and through us is to accuse us in the

> courts of heaven. His function is a legal one against us. To further emphasize this, 1 Peter chapter 5, verse 8 says we have an adversary seeking to devour us. This word "adversary" is the Greek word antidikos and it means an opponent in a lawsuit. Clearly, satan understands that the battle and conflict is a legal one. We must understand it as well.
>
> If we are going to get our "kingdom prayers" answered, we must realize we have to "win" in the courts of heaven first. The battle is a legal battle where we silence the accuser who has built a case to hold territory. We take the blood of Jesus and use His sacrifice to remove every legal right the devil has to resist us. This is a legal process in the spirit realm. Once this is done we can then march to the battlefield and win every time.

His illustration on this matter signifies a suitable understanding for what is actually going on when legal rights are involved.

To understand this portion of the courtroom type-judicial system in heaven, it is also important to understand the place of Kingship and priesthood that we hold in the Kingdom system of heaven. The two are closely related when dealing with breaking legal rights, and then battling that which is in the way thereafter. I like to see it as a formal system with branches interweaving throughout the entire two part collaboration. The courtroom being the first in this collaboration, spiritual warfare and asserting authority given being the second, and discernment, prayer, and fasting as some interweaving principals throughout.

Every system and assertion God has for us, is because of His love for us. I firmly believe that when we gain an understanding of the judicial system in heaven, as well as seek His Kingdom, which are both necessary to succeed any type of adversary and opposition; it is a simple way to get more intimate with Him. To understand, we must read His word. To gain authority we must ask Him who holds it. To triumph over the legal rights held against us by satan, we must pray with persistance to Jesus and enter into a place of humility and relationship. Although these things are simple in concept, they are not as simple to accomplish. There are a few reasons this isn't as simple to do as it is to understand. First, satan's demons are constantly there trying to distract us from the root cause of any of our problems. Second, in order to have Jesus Christ's authority, we must have Him living in us, coursing through our veins, knowing the mission we have to complete. Thirdly, we have to know this history found in the written word to understand not only the title of a priest, but also the role to become a priest like Christ. Each of these endeavors takes passion and time. We actually have to spend time getting to know Jesus to use His authority, otherwise, we may end up like the exorcist Jews in Acts. We have to spend time praying persistently while seeking His will. This too is an act of selflessness and humility, not easily attained if we're bogged down by demons. I hope that this helps depict part of the process that is involved with being set free in deliverance from deeper-rooted demons and legal rights they may hold.

When we make proactive movements of defensive praying leading to deliverance, we are making room for Jesus to work. This will be more than a necessary tool when the antichrist and false prophet begin to appear in the world as the familiar reading in revelation tells us they will. According to the prophecies throughout the bible regarding the things Christians will have to endure in the end times after the antichrist power begins to rise, we must be as ready as possible. In these times to come, if Jesus has taken the very demons that once put us in agreement with our enemy, then we will have a more pure, more capable, undiluted ability of thoroughly hearing the voice of God, and effectively doing His will. He will use His people in these times to make sure all is in place for His arrival as the bridegroom. Following the antichrist, the false prophet will propel the serious persecutions on the Christian people into action. He will slyly force and manipulate the worship of the image of the beast., taking his mark. This will allow hearing God's voice clearly to ensure survival. This will allow helping others deal with what will be very scary for most. It will also allow for a triumphant victory over satan and his strategy simply by not being in the same territory as the enemy. This territory will be a literal geographical place or places to avoid at all costs, but also a spiritual plane if you will. When demons manifest more regularly on earth as actual physical creatures in this time, we will by God's direction of righteousness through deliverance, have the ability to persevere through some of the most trying persecutions. Perhaps completely avoid them and dwell under the shadow of God. With deliverance and freedom from the maneuvers of unclean spirits, we may be able to dwell in safety with Him. The New International Version of Psalm 91:1 says it best: ***Whoever dwells in the shelter of the Most High will rest in the shadow of the Almighty.***

I've learned that the best part of deliverance is watching the lives of people change as they walk in their new freedom. It is watching the peace of God cover them. Deliverance is the full spectrum of authority in Christ, being used to demolish our enemy. Can we as a holy people, please stop bypassing important gifts that God deliberately gave to us? Can we as a righteous and blessed people pray for understanding on the end times that are coming sooner than we think? Can we as a church body teach others the truth of the gospels of Jesus Christ, partaking of all the gifts God gave us? It is in these days that we must be fully armed, physically and spiritually. As Noah prepared an ark for the flood, so too must we prepare for the coming of the Savior of the world. In this preparation we must listen! We must obey! We must know His voice! We must desire to know His concerns and wants more than any impeding prayers and desires for ourselves. This is on a global, eternal perspective. The biggest revival known to man will shortly hit the world, and to be a part of it, we must be holy in His authority to not be deceived by the darkness that is also coming. If we are walking with Him in His holiness, authority, and kingship, then we will soar into new heights of anointing and actions of Christ Himself.

I realize that the majority of the people reading this book may already do these things, but I implore you to specifically ask Jesus for instruction for the end times. Simply ask Him for wisdom on the matter, for it is near. It is upon us, and we must be sober in mind, spirit and body. We must walk with Christ in this last hour, for when it falls, it will fall hard. This will not be a time to prepare, or learn His voice, rather, it will be a time to walk in all that He has prepared you for already. The books in the Bible make things clear as to how these days will come upon us if we take the time to study.

It is not that we are weak or that we have a constant influence from demons around us, on us, or in us, but it is because we are great. We have everything that Christ had, making us a threat to satan. He knows he is already defeated, but he will do his best to take down each and every child of God. We must be on guard, sober, and ready to fight at a moments notice. I am not just talking about for other Christians that are being affected somehow. I am also speaking of ourselves. A couple times a month, it is pointed out to me that I need some form of deliverance. God always makes it clear to me because I will feel far from Him, or other times, I will feel differently inside; and not for the better. These traits that can show up, unwanted and unannounced are inevitably a demon. These things can manifest in many ways as I hope I have explained sufficiently.

You must be willing to take an honest look at yourself from the inside out, in order to allow God to remove them and allow freedom to become a lifestyle. I mostly do this alone, as deliverance can be embarrassing or ineffective if others are around. It has been referred to as "self deliverance," because you are alone when doing it, but it can never truly be done alone because Christ is the actual minister. It always begins with an awareness of self. For example, I recently woke up with a heavy heart and began to ask God to help me change my life. Throughout the day I noticed a sadness that made me want to cry. I noticed the following day that I wanted to sleep more than usual and that I wasn't really excited about my day, or life for that matter. I prayed my normal prayers in the morning and at night, but throughout the day, I wasn't feeling very close to God. I didn't have the urge to talk to Him, or pray in tongues as I normally did. Understand that demons will do their very best to distract you from realizing that they are influencing you and that you are in need of deliverance. They will send every hurdle and annoyance to deter you from recognizing that you are one prayer away from intimacy with the Lord.

I am not sure if people are aware of the fact that we can live our whole lives with demons controlling a part of us. We can function as normal human beings, normal citizens, and even normal Christians, yet a part of us is under bondage to a supernatural evil that hungers for the sin. They are hungry, greedy, and relentless creatures, invisible to the naked eye, but nevertheless there. They do not let go easily, and if never confronted, you will live with spirits influencing you forever. There is not a day that goes by that the Lord doesn't pinpoint a demon over someone's life that needs freedom. I want you to understand that no one can avoid it. But we can certainly overcome! God once showed me that these demons hunger for us to sin, to fulfill their own craving for evil, but also to keep us as far from God as possible. They are relentless in their endeavors, feeding off your weaknesses. It is especially dangerous as a Christian. I say this because one of a Christ-follower's jobs is to allow Jesus to transform them. It is so important to completely surrender all to Christ, and if we are consciously doing this to the best of our ability, you would think it would be somewhat simple. I know firsthand that it is not quite this simple. Most don't even realize they have a demon. They may think they struggle with certain things, or know their own weaknesses, but in all reality, it is demonic.

I would like to discuss the possibilities of overcoming demonic influence, however, I would also like to pinpoint what it feels like at the beginning, middle, and end of when a demon is slowly integrating into your everyday life. It begins with sin, of course. Even if you don't read, follow, and believe the Bible as the living breath of God, you too are susceptible to the slow degeneration of life. If we participate in activities that satan likes, then we are opening a little crack in the armor for the devil to infiltrate. These things seem obvious, but for the sake of proving my point, I will touch upon a few of them. Let's first talk about sex. In a world full of sexual embodiment in every area of culture and lifestyle, it is difficult to not see it. As a matter of fact, people have become numb to sexual perversion, and that is the better of the ones that actually support and encourage sexual perversion. Those that knowingly come in complete agreement with perversions that go directly against the very history of the word of God, have been given over to a depraved mind. This is not only a biblical principal but also if you pay attention, you yourself can see it in your own life or maybe a friend or loved one. First let's observe scripture concerning this concept described in Romans 1:25-32 (NET):

> **_25 They exchanged the truth of God for a lie and worshiped and served the creation rather than the Creator, who is blessed forever! Amen. 26 For this reason God gave them over to dishonorable passions. For their women exchanged the natural sexual relations for unnatural ones, 27 and likewise the men also abandoned natural relations with women and were inflamed in their passions for one another. Men committed shameless acts with men and received in themselves the due penalty for their error. 28 And just as they did not see fit to acknowledge God, God gave them over to a depraved mind, to do what should not be done. 29 They are filled with every kind of unrighteousness, wickedness,_**

covetousness, malice. They are rife with envy, murder, strife, deceit, hostility. They are gossips,
30 *slanderers, haters of God, insolent, arrogant, boastful, contrivers of all sorts of evil, disobedient to parents,*
31 *senseless, covenant-breakers, heartless, ruthless.*
32 *Although they fully know God's righteous decree that those who practice such things deserve to die, they not only do them but also approve of those who practice them.*

People that know Him are still continuing to abstain from giving Him thanks. People that know Him are still not giving Him glory while worshipping futile statues that look like human beings. This isn't a far cry from what is still happening in our society today. Without pointing out specific religions as to not offend anyone, can we just observe that some people pray to a man on a cross. While some pray to the Virgin Mary and others are bowing down to gods and goddesses of mother nature, and Shiva. Or, on the what appears to be the darker side of the spectrum, there are those who sacrifice animals to their gods to receive some sort of reward for their work. Although this seems darker due to the killing of something, it is not. The same devil that pushes people to worship nature, mother earth, lover of all religions and the transformer of peace in any capacity, is the same devil that causes people to sacrifice a chicken, or do a magic spell. Let me be clear about the meaning of worship. According to ***Strong's Concordance*** Hebrew: 5456 the word "sagad: to prostrate oneself (in worship)" while in Aramaic it means be "lowly, submissive, prostrate oneself in prayer, etc." To be lowly and submissive can be perceived through a physical positioning of our bodies, but also a positioning of one's heart. I think that people get confused when we use this word. I think that people aren't even aware that they are worshipping something other the God Himself. Why do I think this? It is too often I hear someone thank "Mother Earth" for the power a women holds. Or others asking the universe for something, walking around professing, advocating and promoting a practice or meditation that changed them. This is still worship.

The one true God, the Creator of the heavens and the earth is a jealous God. This act of worshipping anything but Him will not fly. It is idolatry that leaves a place for satan to lay his devious egg that will hatch into a malevolent demon. Then, it will influence you, and possible thereafter, turn into a stronghold in one's life. And in this deception that is taking humanity, God gives these people over to these powers that they worship. He allows them to go and worship the created rather than the Creator, which eventually leads to complete foolish blindness. I pray this wakes you up, but if you need a little experience to wake you up then I would be happy to assist.

First, let's also look at the people that do not want to give the one true God His glory and acknowledgement I have spoken to so many people that just cannot believe that God has to have a specific name, like the name Jesus, for example. They refuse to believe, for reasons such as color discrimination, history, culture, or science. They just cannot believe that God would have a name. These are blinders that the devil puts over our eyes. It can be a generational, anti-Christ problem stemming from one's family heritage, or it can simply be a lack of knowledge. Either way, you are giving into a fallen nature, walking the earth lost in translation between holiness and worldliness. This is exactly where satan wants us. He will make you think that having sex with anyone you want any time you want, is an empowering trait of independence and sexuality, celebrating freedom. A great example of our society coming into agreement with such sexual deviance are the television and movie industry. And if you follow the spending trend, the pornography industry brings an estimated four billion dollars a year, according to Pornography Statistics: Annual Report 2015[29].

Just to name a couple examples of encouraging this type of immoral behavior, I immediately think of the TV series titled *Sex in the City*. It glorified singlehood by embracing sex and power. Or more recently, the movie, *50 Shades of Gray,* which depicts and glamorizes the idea of supporting sex outside of marriage, and sexual perversion. I know many Christians that watched the movie and have commented that they enjoyed it. How are we, as God's holy people, watching these things which bring a perverted demon into our homes and quite possibly our bodies? You may of course disagree with this idea, but I have had many experiences with myself and other people concerning casting out demons because of a movie or TV show they watched. How do I know that was the exact cause? The demon either told me during the deliverance, or God told me when I was praying for the person to find out what was wrong. So when we take these fictitious forms of expression on our televisions, movies, or internet and make them our own, danger is also at bay. Sexual openness and being one in energy with another person's soul has been taught for centuries. From ancient teachings of Yoga, martial arts, and tantric studies just to name a few, satan has found a way to distort, pervert, and twist the beauty of marriage and monogamy. Now our society has been brainwashed to believe that it is "ok" to have multiple marriages, girlfriends, mistresses, threesomes, full blown orgies and even to become a swinger. . Now none of it is a new concept, to partake of such things has been around forever, but the fact that we somehow think it is ok while adapting it into our life-styles and even adapting it into our children's life-styles is a problem. I see more and more people giving way to these demonic teachings. Unfortunately, even some Christians are lost. Can you believe I have heard people say that it is holy to show love, sexual and otherwise, to numerous women because they are sharing a piece of their god with them through love? This was never what God intended humans to do.

While it is accurate to say as God stated, that when you have sex with a person you become one with them, these practices are missing some very important points. The demons in both people or all people that are having sex, are mingling with one another. They too are enjoying the energy exchange as you so freely celebrate your sexuality because you are now gaining that persons demons. They now have open access to influence you in your life. So if the person you decided to go home with after a sexy night out with the girls, is struggling with pornography and addiction, you now may begin to struggle with the things he is tempted by. Your soul and energies have become one, and so have your demons. I feel that God would like me to briefly touch upon one of the greatest deceptions moving in our world today as expressed in 1 Timothy 4:1 (KJV) ***Now the Spirit speaketh expressly, that in the latter times some shall depart from the faith, giving heed to seducing spirits, and doctrines of devils.***

How can this be? How can people be deceived by

seducing spirits? Perhaps it is by clearing our minds, or doing certain movements that ultimately worship gods from ancient times before Christ was on earth. I am speaking of the practice of Yoga. I realize this is a bit of a controversial topic, but I really wouldn't expect any less when dealing with seducing spirits or teachings from devils. They certainly know what they are doing. They know how to play the human race on their weaknesses of pride desiring to be gods themselves. Also, most deceptive teachings about weight control steer to stroke the ego with vanity while deep breathing is promoted scientifically and therapeutically to reduce stress and reach certain heights of enlightenment. Have any Christians reading this, that practice yoga, ever thought about why their bodies and minds are being uplifted, stretched, energized and broadened simply by doing some movements? Have you ever prayed and asked God what the secret behind yoga really is? A former yoga practitioner, William Downs, describes how this practice actually involves worshipping other gods[30]:

> One branch or path of yoga is called *Hatha Yoga* and this is probably what most people in the West associate with the word "yoga" – believing it is being practiced only for mental and physical health.
>
> Some of the positions in yoga are not quite as harmless as they may appear, but are obviously of occult origin, as in the "cobra", which is usually followed by "greeting the sun" – and taking the pose of the "mountain". These are all positions which are designed to welcome Hindu gods.
>
> In the Hatha Yoga Pradipika it mentions the

following in chapter one:

"Salutations to Shiva, who taught the science of Hatha Yoga. It is the aspirant's stairway to the heights of Raja Yoga... Yogi Svatmarama . . . explains the science of hatha for one reason – Raja Yoga."

So here we see clearly that Hatha Yoga was specifically designed to lead the practitioner onto Raja Yoga. Raja Yoga, however, is chiefly concerned with the cultivation of the mind through meditation.

Shiva is also known as the *Destroyer* (of evil) or Yogeshwara (Lord of Yogis). Shiva's consort is *Devi*, or *Kali*, the goddess of death.

Therefore, the idea that Hatha Yoga is "purely physical" is very much once again a distortion of the truth (in other words, an outright lie) and indeed begs the question, "Why the cover up or confusion?"

This is in the same bracket as martial arts. I always think of Qui Gong because I actually practiced it for a period of time, years ago. These very deliberate movements in correlation with meditation and an empty, clear mind, you have just made a recipe for demons to enter you. I know firsthand, but also can clearly see it all around the world. These movements and practices are very closely related to a false sense of awareness. They tend to give you a false sense of sexuality because of the awareness you are developing within yourself and your body. When in truth, you may be embracing an awareness of positive, but the demons then begin to step in and distortedly twist this perception. It can also be attributed to sexual openness and being one in energy with the another person's soul through sexual intimacy. While this is accurate, as God stated that when you have sex with a person you become one with them, this new-age, ancient concept is leaving something very important out; that your sharing demons. In the same manner, once your eyes have been opened to this deception, cutting all ungodly soul ties with every sexual partner will be of utmost importance in transitioning into your courtship with Christ.

Satan will also use your competitive nature, or your work ethic to entice you into worshipping success. Your career can quickly take the top spot in your life and become a god we worship. He will give you subtle notions and encourage you to work your way to the top of that ladder of success. Making more money will make you happy. If you can just havehat car, or that house, or that position, you can run the world. I am not saying that a dedicated, work ethic isn't a good thing. God says in Colossians 3:23 (NET) ***Whatever you are doing, work at it with enthusiasm, as to the Lord and not for people.***

I believe it is very important to do everything with joy, knowing it is for God. That includes work and work morals, however, if it begins to take the place of your relationship with God, then you're headed exactly where the devil wants you. Anything that takes away from the structure of worshipping the one true God, is where satan will be. Now please don't misunderstand, there is power in what he does. If you're a musician that has given non intentional, or intentional worship to the devil, your music could very well supersede any other singer or musician. Your lyrics will flow out of your mouth without hesitation. People will awe over your skill and talent.

There are two views I hold on this. First, gifts and talents come from God. They were given to you before you were even formed in your mother's womb. So I am not trying to take away anyone's God given talents. However, there sometimes comes a point when someone gives himself over to such an ungodly mess of satan and his demons that their skill begins to accelerate, but the glory will go to them, to their producer or manager. The glory will go to anyone but God. Demonic overtones can begin to weave in and out of someone's skill. If you dance it may become sexual in nature or take on attributes of movements from ancient foreign god-worship. If you rap, your lyrics may be full of a worldly view focusing on issues or situations that have to do only with selfishness. If you run a business it will become about fulfilling desires or whatever your wants and needs are. There is a common thread within each situation that involves the devil; they are distraction and deception. If you think that anything in your life is more important than glorifying Christ and leading others to salvation to freely receive eternal life with God, why then my friend, you have been duped.

As these lies and deceptions creep their way into your life, they begin to block your moments with the one true God. They begin to place a veil over your eyes causing you to see twisted things as acceptable and correct. I have actually been there, so I am not speaking as some holier-than-thou person. It is from my experiences that allow me to write such things with confidence in knowing the validity of these truths. Because I have been through these things, I would like to offer a solution to all of you. I would like for everyone reading this, Christian, non- Christian, and even satanists, to hear these words and teachings, for I believe it will change your life; dramatically transforming you into the beautifully made human being that God intended you to be. Please understand that I have no selfish gain in writing this book. It is part of my calling to prepare people, as God allows, for the end of the world. It is my job to prepare people spiritually for this beautiful day, and in so doing, this book was birthed. God has stripped from me everything that I once relied on that would just not suit following the Holiest of Holies. In doing this, He taught me that no challenge is big enough to ever defeat me. This is not because of my own strength, but because of His. I relied on smoking, drinking, sex, anger, manipulation and fear to run my life, but when He took each of these things from me, He replaced them with Himself. His spirit permeates throughout my body emanating His truth and love to all that are around me. This is not some delusion. This is not some tactic to get you to believe or convince you of anything. It is simply fact.

My prayer is that you will take time to make an assessment of where you are spiritually, commit to deepening your relationship with God, and remove anything that is hindering you from becoming all that God created you to be. By asking and allowing Jesus to remove the demonic influences in your life, you will open the door to the heavenly realm and an eternity with Him. To help you along, here is a prayer that you can say aloud, in your personal time, that can be a beginning to your life of freedom with deliverance administered by Jesus. If you have not accepted Jesus Christ as your Lord and savior, I would suggest strongly that you receive that honor now. Receiving His salvation first is important so that you have the power of His Holy Spirit living inside of you to remove the unclean spirits. May God bless you on this amazing journey!

Deliverance Prayer: Derik Prince's Prayer[31]:

This is a very effective prayer used by Derik Prince at his conferences on deliverance. Many People have used it with good results. Pray it out loud over yourself and all those with you.

Lord Jesus Christ, I believe that you are the son of God and the only way to God, that you died on the cross for my sins and rose again from the dead. I come to you now for mercy and for forgiveness. I believe you do forgive me and receive me as your child. And because you receive me, I receive myself as a child of God and now Lord you know the special problem that I have, the demonic influences that torment me. Lord, I want to meet your conditions and receive your deliverance. First of all, I forgive every other person, whoever harmed me or wronged me. (Pause for a moment and have everyone quietly name the persons they need to forgive to themselves.) [I forgive them all now.]

Lord, I have forgiven all these persons. I have laid down all bitterness, all resentment, all hatred and all rebellion. I believe you have forgiven me. I thank you for it. I also renounce every contact with satan, with occult power, with secret societies, and with anything in satan's territory. I repent of being on that territory and I turn my back on it now. Also Lord, if there is a curse over my life, I thank you that on the cross you were made a curse that I may be redeemed from the curse and receive the blessing and I claim that now. Released from the curse, and entering into the blessing. And now Lord, I want to come against any evil spirit in me, that occupies any area of my life or personality. I want to tell you that I hate them! They are my enemies! I will not make peace with them, they are my enemies, I will not make peace with them, I will not compromise with them, they will have no more place in me. I turn against them now and in the authority of your name Jesus, I command them to leave me. I expel them right now in the name of Jesus, Amen.

Leader now prays this out loud over everyone:

Now Lord as your servant and representative under authority of the local leadership, I take dominion in Jesus' name. Release these people now. I affirm that Jesus Christ is Lord over this gathering, that He has defeated satan, that He holds the keys of death and of Hades, that all authority has been given to Him in Heaven and on earth. Satan you are subject to us, you have to go from these people, you have no option. The Bible says you must leave in the name of Jesus, Amen.

Scripture References for Demonic Spirits:

Spirit of infirmity or weakness (Luke 13:11), Spirit of Antichrist (I John 4:3), Spirit of fear (II Tim. 1:7), Deaf spirit (Mark 9:25), Perverse spirit (Isa. 19:14), Dumb spirit (Mark 9:25), Sorrowful spirit (I Sam. 1:15), Blind spirit (Matt. 9:27), Spirit of slumber (Rom. 11:8), Foul spirit (Mark 9:25; Rev. 18:2), Spirit of whoredoms (Hos. 5:4), Unclean spirit (Matt. 14:43; Mark 1:23, 26; 3:30; 5:2,8, 7:25), Destroying spirit (Deut. 13:15), Evil spirit (Judges 9:23; I Sam. 16:14-16, 23; 18:10; 19:9), Spirit of divination (Acts 16:16), Another spirit (II Cor. 11:4), Spirit of bondage (Rom. 8:15), Hasty of spirit (Prov. 14:29), Spirit of error (I John 4:6), Haughty spirit (Prov. 16:18), Spirit of false doctrines (Ex. 23:1; Matt. 16:12), Perverse spirit (Isa. 19:14), Spirit of jealousy (Num. 5:14), Seducing spirits (I Tim. 4:1), Sad spirit (I Kings 21:5), Jealous spirit (Num. 5:14, 30), Wounded spirit (Prov. 18:14), Lying spirit (I Kings 22:22-23; II Ch. 18:21-22), Proud in spirit (Ecc. 7:8), Spirit of burning (Isa. 4:4), Familiar spirit (Lev. 20:27; I Sam. 28:7-8; I Ch. 10:13; II Ch. 33:6), Spirit of Egypt (Isa. 19:3), Spirit of heaviness (Isa. 61:3), Spirit of unclean devil (Luke 4:33), Spirit of the world (I Cor. 2:12)

http://www.demonbuster.com/howtoid6.html

ABOUT THE AUTHOR

In this innovative revelatory book, Kristina Murawski not only shares some of the most intimate secrets from God's own heart, but also deep secrets given to us through the word of God. She speaks of the very authority to war with the enemy at hand. As she describes with fervor and passion some of her unique experiences that God allowed her to endure, along with many teachings on our enemies, and their power and strategies, she will help to give a new perspective and detailed survival tool kit for your spiritual needs in the darkest days yet to reach the earth.

The Spiritual Survival Kit for the End Times, is a supernatural, yet hands, on practical guide to freedom and protection for the times of the Apocalypse. You will not be fooled. You will not be defeated. You will only triumph with God as the remaining years unfold the prophetic happenings of doom.

- Remove all hindrances keeping you from freedom
- Engage with the Spirit of the living God
- Take authority over demons
- Gain authority and Kingship here on earth

Kristina takes the sometimes difficult topics of the supernatural realm, demons and war, to a whole new level of understanding with revelation from the living God, transformed into a simple blue print for the times at hand. As a born again believer in the Holy God of Israel, Kristina Murawski is propelled to teach, heal and evangelize to all races, cultures, and people. Kristina challenges yet helps all those who are hesitant or fearful of these sometimes difficult topics for Christians, Catholics, Jews, Muslims, Atheists, and all other notions of religion. This riveting book will open your eyes to an unseen world that is meant for your taking.

[1] ***New Wilson's Old Testament Word Studies***, 3rd Edition. Wilson, William. © 1987 by Kregel Publications, a division of Kregel, Inc..

[2] Hope for the Heart. *A Letter from June on Trials.* http://www.hopefortheheart.org/july-2013-letter-from-june-on-trials/. July 2013

[3] https://en.wikipedia.org/wiki/Astrolatry. Jan. 29, 2017

[4] The diary of Colonel Joseph Hyde Pratt, *What were the living conditions in Trench Warfare*. Page 79. http://trenchwarfareworldwar1.weebly.com/living-conditions.html Jan. 29.2017

BIBLIOGRAPHY END NOTES:

[5] *Attack on Pearl Harbor.* Wikipedia. https://en.wikipedia.org/wiki/Attack_on_Pearl_Harbor. Jan. 29, 2017

[6] *Pearl Harbor Day of Infamy* Military. Com http://www.military.com/navy/pearl-harbor.html. Jan. 29, 2017.

[7] Kathryn Kuhlman. Jan. 29, 2017. https://www.canecreekchurch.org/what-s-your-legacy/33-kathryn-kuhlman

[8] Entropy. Jan. 29, 2017. https://www.vocabulary.com/dictionary/entropy

[9] *Entropy in the Old Creation: Is the Universe Running Down?* Jan. 31, 2017. http://www.ldolphin.org/thermod.html

[10] *Evolutionism Vs Creationism,* Just Christian News, Jan. 30, 2017.
http://justchristiannews.com/index.php/2016/11/09/evolution-vs-creationism-2/

[11] *All Hell Breaks Loose. (Revelation 9:1-21).* Jan. 29.2017. https://bible.org/seriespage/18-all-hell-breaks-loose-revelation-91-21

[12] http://whatistranshumanism.org/

[13] Let us Reason Ministries. Jan. 29, 2017. http://www.letusreason.org/Doct11.htm

[14] Wikipedia. Jan. 29.2017. https://home.cern/about

[15] Wikipedia. Jan. 29.2017. https://de.wikipedia.org/wiki/Saint-Genis-Pouilly

[16] *Integrated DNA Technologies,* Jan. 29, 2017. www.idtdna.com

[17] *Baal, Ashtoreth and Molech - God's Old Testament rivals.* Gregory Elder. Jan. 11, 2007.
http://www.redlandsdailyfacts.com/article/ZZ/20070111/NEWS/701119928

[18] Jan, 29, 2017. http://www.jesus-is-savior.com/False%20Religions/Wicca%20&%20Witchcraft/bohemian_moloch.htm

[19] Jan. 29, 2017. http://www.jesus-is-savior.com/False%20Religions/Wicca%20&%20Witchcraft/bohemian_grove_exposed.htm

[20] *Transcendental Magic,* Eliphas Levi, Jan. 30, 2017
https://archive.org/stream/transcendentalma00leviuoft/trans

cendentalma00leviuoft_djvu.txt

[21] *The True Masonic Order.* Henry Epps, Jan. 30, 2017. http://symboldictionary.net/?p=1143

[22] Wikipedia, Jan. 30, 2017. https://en.wikipedia.org/wiki/Baphomet

[23] Vigilant Reports in *The Opening Ceremony of the World's Largest Tunnel Was a Bizarre Occult Ritual. Jan. 30, 2017.* http://vigilantcitizen.com/vigilantreport/opening-ceremony-worlds-largest-tunnel-bizarre-occult-ritual/

[24] *Palmyra's Arch of Triumph recreated in Trafalgar Square.* Jan, 30, 2017. https://www.theguardian.com/culture/2016/apr/19/palmyras-triumphal-arch-recreated-in-trafalgar-square

[25] Jan. 30, 2017. http://www.medievalcollectibles.com/c-952-roman-gladius-swords.aspx)

[26] Jan. 30, 2017. https://en.wikipedia.org/wiki/Pugio

[27] Strong's Hebrew: 1245. בָּקַשׁ (baqash) to seek. Bible Hub. Jan. 30, 2017. biblehub.com/hebrew/1245.htm

[28] *Kingdom Prayers to Win in the Courts of Heaven,* Charisma News, Robert Henderson. Nov. 1, 2014 www.charismanews.com/.../45956-kingdom-prayers-to-win-in-the-courts-of-heaven

[29] Pornography Statistics: Annual Report © 2015 Covenant Eyes | Legal http://www.covenanteyes.com/pornstats/

[30] The Spiritual Deception of Yoga. William Downs. April 21, 2010. Christian Assemblies International. http://www.cai.org/testimonies/spiritual-deception-yoga

[31] Derik Prince's Prayer. Jan. 31, 2017. http://the-truth-will-set-you-free.org/2.html

Made in the USA
Columbia, SC
02 July 2022